Community Under Anarchy

Community Under Anarchy

Transnational Identity and the Evolution of Cooperation

Bruce Cronin

COLUMBIA UNIVERSITY PRESS   NEW YORK

COLUMBIA UNIVERSITY PRESS
Publishers Since 1893
New York   Chichester, West Sussex
Copyright © 1999 Columbia University Press

Library of Congress Cataloging-in-Publication Data

Cronin, Bruce, 1957–
    Community under anarchy: transnational identity and the evolution
of cooperation / Bruce Cronin.
        p.   cm.
    Includes bibliographical references and index.
    ISBN 0-231-11596-2.—ISBN 0-231-11597-0 (pbk.)
    1. International cooperation.   2. International relations.
3. Group identity.   I. Title.
JZ1318.C76 1999
327.1'7—dc21   99-10733
                                                                  CIP

Casebound editions of Columbia University Press books are printed on permanent
and durable acid-free paper.

Printed in the United States of America
c 10 9 8 7 6 5 4 3 2 1
p 10 9 8 7 6 5 4 3 2 1

For Trevor

Contents

Acknowledgments

This book is not only the product of my own research and thinking but also the product of the intellectual communities within which I have had the fortune to work. I gratefully acknowledge the assistance, support, and pointed criticism that I received while a graduate student, post-doctoral fellow, and assistant professor at Columbia University, Harvard University, and the University of Wisconsin-Madison, respectively.

Specifically, John Ruggie, Jack Snyder, Hendrick Spruyt, and Robert Jervis were key figures in helping me to conceptualize and reconceptualize the project. They were also careful and perceptive readers. Sammy Barkin and Tami Stukey helped me through the early stages as well. Alex Wendt was an intellectual inspiration and a superb critical reader of my theory chapters. Michael Barnett has been a good friend and invaluable colleague whose criticism and helpful suggestions made me rethink major sections of the book. Joe Lepgold also provided very useful comments and advice on various portions of the manuscript.

I also benefited from the comments of Henry Nau and Glen Chaffetz. Patricia Moynagh's extensive knowledge of political theory and keen insights helped to enrich my thinking and ultimately made this a better work. Kate Wittenberg was essential for shepherding me through the review process. Without her continued support and advice, the outcome would have been different. I also enjoyed working with Susan Pensak, senior manuscript editor at Columbia University Press. Finally, I acknowledge the helpful comments and suggestions by three anonymous reviewers. This was clearly a case where the review process greatly improved the final product.

Research support has been provided by the Olin Institute/Center for International Affairs, the Wisconsin Alumni Research Fund, and the John D. and Catherine T. MacArthur Foundation.

I appreciate the opportunity to have presented various portions of this book at academic seminars and forums over the past few years, including the American Political Science Association, the University of Wisconsin Global Studies Research Program, the Yale University International Relations Seminar, and the International Studies Association.

Community Under Anarchy

Part 1

Theory and Concepts

1   *The Concept of Transnational Communities*

In a world of independent sovereign states it is often difficult to conceive of a community beyond the protective walls of national borders. Indeed, in the field of international relations the term *community* rarely appears either as a theoretical concept or descriptive phrase.[1] For most of the literature, the lack of a central authority and common world culture precludes the formation of transnational communities. As a result, the only alternative to the extremes of perpetual war and world government is cooperation, defined in terms of mutual adjustment of policies in the pursuit of well-defined but limited goals.[2] Realists tend to focus on alliances as the primary form of cooperation, while institutionalists examine regimes and other types of institutions. Neither, however, sees a foundation for cohesive communities among sovereign states. States can have shared interests, but not shared identities.

This book seeks to build such a foundation. It explains how political elites construct transnational communities by developing common social identities. These identities are the fundamental building blocks of the community. My primary focus in this regard are the types of security arrangements states create that are based on principles of group cohesion. These include concert systems, pluralistic security communities, amalgamated security communities, common security associations, and collective security systems. In developing this theme the book illustrates how states distinguish friends from enemies, partners from competitors, and communities from outsiders, beyond political expediency.

My claim is the following: transnational political communities form when a set of political actors sharing a common social characteristic, a common relationship, a common experience, and a positive interdependence develop a political consciousness that defines them as a unique group. This is facilitated by the creation of conceptual distinctions between a notion of self and other, for example, East-West, democratic-autocratic, great power–secondary power, Old World–New World. The *type* of transnational identity (the independent variable) determines the type of cohesive security arrangement (the dependent variable). Thus, for example, a common identity among great powers will lead to a concert system. None of this requires the formation of a world government or a transformation of the anarchic environment. In making this argument I do not deny the powerful polarizing effects of anarchy and sovereignty, but rather I examine the conditions under which these effects can be overcome. In doing so I draw on recent advances in social theory, particularly constructivist approaches in international relations, symbolic interactionist sociology, and social identity theory.

I begin with the premise that communities require some degree of group cohesion and a shared sense of self. However, they do not require a formal centralized political authority to maintain them. They can be tightly knit (for example, tribal societies) or loosely constructed (for example, professional associations). They can consist of individuals or corporate entities. I define community as a collectivity of political actors organized on the basis of a common good and a shared sense of self, giving its members a positive stake in building and maintaining internal relationships.[3] The notion of a common good and shared sense of self distinguishes community from other forms of association. *Political* communities are those that are concerned with the allocation of values or resources. The types of communities with which I am concerned are those that are voluntarily constructed by state elites based on a recognition that they share a special relationship to the other members. This constructivist notion stands in contrast to the communitarian concept, which views community as something organic, which one is born into and grows within.[4] My use of community, on the other hand, requires a political consciousness. Therefore, my definition is somewhat analogous to Rousseau's general will, which is volunteerist but presupposes a group awareness of a common good.[5]

A transnational community is one that transcends juridical borders. It can be formed between societal actors (such as a workers' international or international Catholicism) or between states (represented by their respective ruling coalitions). In this book I am primarily interested in the latter. I prefer the term *trans*national to *inter*national because this shifts the emphasis away from individually based bilateral relationships between states toward group dynamics.[6] The concept of international suggests a relationship between two or more distinct independent entities, while the idea of transnational implies transcending traditional boundaries. In this sense a transnational community has an existence that is independent of the states that comprise it.

This book examines the social foundations of transnational communities by focusing on the key element in their formation: the development of common identities shared by the member states. Such transnational identities transcend the barriers that separate sovereign states. According to a standard dictionary definition, identities are sets of behavioral or personal characteristics by which an individual is recognizable as a member of a group.[7] In chapter 2 I will expand this definition to incorporate sociological concepts. Social identities are those parts of the self-concept that are derived from the social categories with which one is associated (for example, American or professor). Transnational identities are social identities that transcend juridical borders (for example, great power or European state).

Structural theories tend to minimize the importance of identity as an explanatory variable because the anarchic environment does not permit any major variation in state behavior. The system conditions the form of interaction that occurs between states, but interaction cannot change the structure of the system. Thus, for analytical purposes, a state is a state and only the strategic environment varies.[8] As a result, neorealism's emphasis on security and survival reduces all states to their primal characteristics. Yet as E. H. Carr observes, consistent realism excludes four elements that are essential to all political thinking: a finite goal (beyond self-preservation), an emotional appeal, a right of moral judgment, and a ground for action.[9] By offering an understanding of self in relation to others, identities can address these basic existential issues and, further, provide grounds for purposive or meaningful action.

To the extent that identities are viewed as exclusive, they are unit-level attributes and can explain state parochialism better than they can transnational community. However, while the principle of sovereignty creates political and psychological boundaries that separate one society from another, sovereignty does not mean social autonomy. States continually interact with, influence, and occasionally emulate each other. Often this process serves to highlight and strengthen the boundaries that divide them, however, it can also diminish them. In developing a theory of transnational identity in chapter 2, I will examine the conditions under which transnational identities can transform a parochial definition of self and interest to one based on membership in a conceptual social group. These groups form the basis of transnational communities and provide the theoretical foundation for variation in security arrangements under anarchy.

Anarchy and the Barriers to Community

Traditionally, the menu for choice of international security arrangements has been limited. Most of the security literature proceeds from the assumption that the lack of a central authority in the international environment breeds insecurity, mistrust, and fear. For both realists and neorealists, in particular, states are predisposed toward self-help and parochialism and resist efforts to become entangled in any relationship that significantly limits their freedom of action. From this perspective there can be only three possible security arrangements: a perpetual war of all against all (an international state of nature), a balance of power system, and a world government or empire. Since the latter would require a transformation of the anarchical environment, this possibility can be eliminated so long as independent sovereign states exist.

This leaves us with perpetual war and a balance of power. For neorealism, the former can also be eliminated because the logic of the latter (as well as the frequent introduction of hegemony into the system) provides a measure of stability and order. Rational states wishing to survive form alliances to enhance their capabilities through combination with others. This reduces incentives to initiate war since the prospects for victory are uncertain. As a result, we are left only with a balance of power system, which Waltz argues exists in any anarchic order whether it be comprised of nation-states, city-states, or even street gangs.[10] In such a system the distribution of material capabilities is the key variable for understanding and explaining diplomatic history. It tells us whether the system will be bipolar or multipolar, which states will dominate, and whose interests will be served in the international order.

In such an environment there is no basis upon which to build communities among states, since strategic calculation makes all other states both potential allies and potential adversaries. The segmentation of the world into independent nation-states creates a situation whereby each unit not only determines its own interests autonomously but also must provide its own means to pursue them.[11] Sovereignty places a wall between one's society and all others. For these reasons, neorealist theories argue that deep structure (anarchy) generates observable patterns of behavior in the system that are limited to balancing, competition, and egoism. Thus neorealists posit an ongoing struggle for power and wealth as a "law" of international politics in an environment of unregulated competition.[12]

How, then, can one speak of community in international politics? The simple answer is, we cannot so long as we accept this model of the international environment. The crucial task is to demonstrate that deep structure is a powerful but not determining factor in influencing state behavior. Institutionalists do so by arguing that anarchy places strong but not insurmountable restrictions on cooperation. For institutionalists, states can create functional institutions to achieve mutual gains without a prior transformation of the anarchic environment. In particular, regime theories show how a convergence of self-interest between states can facilitate cooperation in defined issue areas, when independent action would result in pareto-inferior outcomes.[13] Moreover, they demonstrate how institutions can help to overcome collective action problems, uncertainty, and mistrust, all key barriers to cooperation posited by realists. Most important, institutionalists argue that an anarchic environment is not necessarily zero-sum and there are therefore opportunities for mutual gain. This can lead to a variety of patterns of interactions between states.[14]

While this can explain cooperation in international politics, it cannot in and of itself account for the formation of transnational communities, primarily because these theories do not posit any circumstances under which its regimes and institutions can transform the social environment through which states interact. Interaction is generally presented as a dichotomous variable, cooperation or conflict, rather than as a continuum that could enable us to differentiate between forms of cooperation. Building an alliance and engaging in multilateral security management are both forms of cooperation. However, they produce very different types of security arrangements. Shared interests are necessary but not sufficient elements for building transnational communities. Without a corresponding shared sense of being, that is, a social identity, relationships remain ad hoc and opportunistic. While regimes can facilitate trust and encourage reciprocity, they do not create a sense of group cohesion, another necessary element in any type of community. Thus regime theory cannot tell us the conditions under which a balance of power system could be transformed into a more cohesive security arrangement, such as a collective security system or a concert of great powers.

To understand the various forms of cooperation that can develop within the anarchic environment, we need to shift our focus away from structural variables toward an examination of interstate relationships. The structure of relationships provides a social arrangement of the units that is based not on material capabilities but on conceptions of self. For this line of argument, the constructivist critique is most helpful. Constructivists argue that Waltz's definition of structure cannot predict the content or dynamics of anarchy; different forms of unit interaction can produce different types of systems. This is based on the premise that the dynamics of international politics is neither natural nor given by deep structure, but rather is socially constructed by political actors through their interactions and relationships.[15] Thus, the condition of anarchy allows for a wide variety of behaviors that are determined not by the imperatives of structure but by the way in which political actors perceive their situations and their social environment. Constructivism, then, offers an intersubjective element as well as a redefinition of structure.[16]

In an influential critique of Waltz Alexander Wendt argues that one cannot derive self-help or balancing behavior from the principle of anarchy alone. He holds that without prior assumptions about the structure of identities in the system Waltz's materialist definition of structure is indeterminate of behavior.[17] He brings the interaction of the units back into the systems model by demonstrating that state actors and systemic structures are mutually constitutive. If self-help is not a constitutive feature of anarchy, he argues that it must emerge causally from processes in which anarchy plays only a permissive role.[18] Therefore, international anarchy does not constitute a single form with relatively fixed features but rather is a condition within which many variations can be arranged.[19] This allows for the formation of transnational communities without a prior transformation of the anarchical environment.

Constructing Security Arrangements

Building from these premises, I posit at least seven possible types of security arrangements that can develop within an anarchic system of states: an international state of nature, a balance of power system, a pluralistic security community, a collective security system, a concert system, a common security association, and an amalgamated security community. The latter five constitute types of transnational political communities. These different types of arrangements can be identified by three primary characteristics, which serve to distinguish one from the others: their constitutive rules, patterns of behavior, and types of institutions governing them.

Constitutive rules are the grammar of action that creates or defines new forms of behavior by providing a "vocabulary" (a stock of meaningful actions or symbols) for international communication.[20] As such they make action meaningful and intelligible to the political actors. While material resources such as military power, tradable goods, and technology provide the *capability* for political and social action, rules and norms provide the framework of meaning through which use of that capability becomes recognizable as purposive policy. This enables political actors to build social relationships with each other and, moreover, to determine which ones will be adversarial and which will be cooperative.

From the rules that constitute and define the system, states create regulative rules that provide a standard from which they can generate expectations, evaluate the behavior of others, and determine the legitimate range of actions that may be undertaken. The patterns of behavior associated with these processes are derived from these rules. To the extent that we can associate certain types of behavior with certain kinds of security arrangements, behavior is a variable. The regularity of behavior and the constitutive rules that underlie the system leads to the development of specific types of institutions.[21] The types of institutions that help to maintain and reproduce the system can also be associated with specific arrangements.

I argue that the type or lack of identities that states develop within a system determines the type of security arrangements they construct. Chapter 2 will build a model that supports this argument. For the moment, this is offered as a hypothesis.

A total lack of any common identity (even as states) will produce an *international state of nature*. This form by definition has no constitutive rules and as such lacks any social or political institutions. The distribution of territory among competing authorities is arbitrary and unstable, a function of power and opportunity, and there is no mutual recognition of borders. Thus, it does not even meet the minimal conditions that would allow for the development of a balance of power system. This is a pure self-help environment. This condition has never existed in the modern world despite the lack of a central authority at the global level, although the environment in Europe during the early Middle Ages loosely approximated this.[22]

A common statist identity in the absence of any other commonalities will produce a *balance of power system*. Such a system is premised on the notion that the survival of state independence requires that no single state predominate. The constitutive rule of the system is the principle of sovereignty, defined in terms of constitutional independence.[23] This provides for a set of stable expectations concerning the distribution of territory and institutional authorities. While Waltz and other realists require only a survival instinct among a plurality of states to maintain a balance of power, without the constitutive principle of sovereignty there can be no concept of statehood, since internationally recognized borders would be absent. Thus it would be difficult to know when a violation has occurred that would spark a balancing alliance.

Balancing and bandwagoning are the primary forms of behavior, and alliances are the main institution for maintaining the system. While a balance of power is in many ways a self-help system, the need to rely on allies for survival also creates a level of security interdependence among the states. Although it is not based on any principle of group cohesion, this system does require an intersubjective agreement concerning the nature of the units (states, as opposed to other types of political actors). Without these prior assumptions, it would be difficult if not impossible to know against whom one is to balance and with whom one is to ally. Moreover, since it is in the interest of all states to support the institution of sovereign statehood against competing authorities, there is a common "statist" identity based on mutual recognition of the units. The survival of one's state requires the survival of the state system and the principle of sovereignty.

A balance of power system and an international state of nature are both examples of competitive self-help security arrangements. As such, they are individualist in both foundation and practice. While there is a vast literature on balance of power systems, far less has been written about what I term community-based security arrangements. This book will deal with three of them: concert systems, common security associations, and amalgamated security communities.

Concerts are multilateral institutions for high-level diplomatic collaboration between the great powers.[24] In a concert system the mutually recognized great powers combine to collectively manage security affairs within a given region. Issues of systemic importance, even those of vital interest to a particular member, are expected to be collectively discussed. Any action taken must be either approved or initiated by the group.[25] Because this requires such a high level of commitment, sacrifice, and trust, the great powers need to develop a relationship that goes beyond cooperation on the basis of mutual self-interest. There must be some concept of a common (that is, group) good. I therefore argue that concert systems require a transnational great power identity based on a mutual recognition that the members constitute a unique and exclusive group with special rights and responsibilities for systems management.

Another type of community-based security arrangement is what I call a *common security association*.[26] Unlike alliances, they are not formed to enhance state capabilities through combination with others in opposition to a specific adversary. Rather, their purpose is to express solidarity among states seeking to promote and legitimize a specific form of political organization or ideology. Within a common security association security is defined in terms of protecting a particular institution such as monarchy, communism, or democracy. Such an arrangement is premised on the idea that national security requires the survival not only of one's own state but of domestic institutions in other states that help to support and legitimize one's own regime. This means banding together against those who would challenge it, particularly transnational revolutionary movements.

The transnational identity that underlies this bond is based on a shared regime type or ideology. This type of arrangement differs from a collective security system in two important ways. First, it is by definition exclusive; only those states promoting the same domestic political institutions or regime are part of the system. Second, its purpose is not to prevent all forms of aggression but only threats to particular institutions. There are many examples of these types of associations: the Nonaligned Movement, the Arab League, the British Commonwealth of Nations, the Holy Alliance, and the Communist International.

A third type of arrangement is an *amalgamated security community* (ASC), characterized by the formal merger of at least two states' administrative, security, and political institutions. In such an arrangement states voluntarily cede their sovereignty to create a new political entity, usually centered around a state that acts as the core. For states to achieve this unusual level of cohesion, there must be a type of shared pan-nationalist identity (either civic or ethnically based). The constitutive rule of such an arrangement is "collectivity as singularity." That is, the collectivity of units acts as a coherent single unit. The pattern of behavior is political integration and the primary institution is a federal government.

This idea of an ASC was first suggested by Karl Deutsch and his associates as a way of understanding the integration of distinct political communities into a single state.[27] However, while their study was informative, they failed to specify a coherent set of variables that would led to the formation of such a community. For example, they concluded that there were twelve conditions (nine "essential" and three that "may be essential") to account for integration. These conditions varied from "a distinctive way of life" to "unbroken links of social communication."[28] What their study lacked was a theory that informed their work and that could connect these random variables. By conceptualizing ASCs as cohesive security arrangements based on a common transnational identity, we can place them in a broader context that would allow for a more coherent set of variables.

ASCs differ somewhat from our conventional notion of security arrangements. Unlike concerts or alliances, for example, amalgamated security communities are not designed to deal with threats as they have been traditionally understood (that is, threats to a country's territorial integrity or sovereignty). However, to the extent that states are the primary institutions that provide security for their societies, the integration of autonomous units under a common political authority represents a distinct form of security arrangement. They are conceptually similar to other types of security mechanisms in the sense that states construct them to protect their populations, institutions, and values. Moreover, they represent a clear choice on the part of the major political actors to promote their security as a single unit rather than through alliance or cooperation with others.

In addition to these three arrangements, there are two other possible community-based systems:

A *pluralistic security community* (PSC) forms when states within an integrated geographic or cognitive area develop a regional identity in which they view their security as linked with that of the region as a whole. Within a PSC states hold stable expectations of peaceful change, facilitated by shared norms, values, and political institutions as well as a high degree of interdependence.[29] Within the region political actors identify and expect their security and welfare to be intimately intertwined with those on the same side of the spatial and cognitive borders. The constitutive rule of PSCs is the peaceful settlement of disputes and peaceful change when required. The patterns of behavior include demilitarization of state armed forces and cooperation in all security matters. The primary institutions facilitating cooperation are regional organizations. The two best examples of this type of arrangement can be found in the North American and European regions after World War II.

A *collective security system* forms when all states within a given system share a cosmopolitan identity that identifies them as members of a single community of nations. Within such a system states not only renounce their right to initiate unilateral military action but also accept obligations to participate in collective action against an aggressor regardless of who it may be.[30] The system is based on the following principles: no grievance warrants resort to force to overturn the status quo, military force is legitimate only to resist attack, and all states have a legal and moral obligation to consider an attack on any nation as an attack upon themselves. The primary constitutive rule is the indivisibility of peace. The defining form of behavior is collective action, and international law and organizations are the primary institutional forms. Unlike a concert system (which only includes great powers) or a pluralistic security community (which is limited to those within a specified region), collective security is nonexclusionary. It requires a very high level of commitment that goes beyond any type of parochial, ethnic, regional, or ideological affinities one may have with others.

The seven models of security arrangements can be compared as follows:

Security System	Common Identity	Constitutive Rules	Patterns of Behavior	Primary Institutions
International State of Nature	None	None	War of all against all	None
Balance of Power System	Statism	Sovereignty and Independence	Balancing and Bandwagoning	Alliances
Concert System	Great Power	Multilateral Security Management	Consultation/ Joint Action	Congresses/ Summits
Pluralistic Security Community	Cognitive Regionalism	Peaceful settlements of disputes	Demilitarization and cooperation	Regional organizations and regimes
Common Security System	Institutional or ideological	Solidarity	Mutual Support	Transnational Association
Amalgamated Security Community	Pan-Nationalism	Collectivity as Singularity	Political Integration	Federal Government
Collective Security System	Cosmopolitan	Peace is indivisible	Collective action	International law and organizations

Organization of the Book

This model places community-based security arrangements within a broader context of possible security systems. How and why cohesive security arrangements evolve during a particular period of history is the focus of this book. Since states can usually promote their strictly parochial interests through self-help policies and alliance-building practices, accounting for other security mechanisms requires a concept of utility that transcends the boundaries of individual units. Chapter 2 develops such a concept based on theories of social identity. The chapter discusses how, why, and under what

conditions social identities can form and how this helps to facilitate transnational relations among political actors. It argues that preferences are
shaped by identities, that political actors can become very attached to these
identities, and that the development of group (transnational) identities can
produce much deeper security cooperation than one would expect from
either a neorealist or neoliberal perspective.

At the same time, if identity is going to be a meaningful explanatory
variable, it must truly be allowed to *vary*. Thus, chapter 2 also examines how
different types of identities can lead to different types of relationships. In
doing so, it lays the foundation for the theme of the book, that the types of
transnational identities determine the types of security systems that develop.

In a practical sense none of this matters if cohesive security arrangements
only form among states that are already predisposed toward close collaboration. One does not need a theory of identity to explain why historic allies
sharing common interests deepen their security ties in the face of a perceived
threat. For this reason, the case studies in part 2 involve states with no
previous history of group cohesion. Chapter 3 examines the rise of a great
power concert (the Concert of Europe) and a common security association
(the Holy Alliance) after 1815 under conditions that strongly favored the
development of a balance of power system. Two powerful states, Britain and
Russia, emerged from the Napoleonic wars as potential adversaries and competitors for European hegemony. The other great powers—Austria, France,
and Prussia—were also traditional rivals with conflicting territorial
ambitions.

None of the states in Europe were democracies in any substantive sense,
therefore we can eliminate the "democratic peace" thesis as an explanation
for group cohesion.[31] Moreover, since the long peace that existed among the
great powers during this period lacked the two conditions commonly cited
to explain this phenomenon during the cold war, bipolarity and nuclear
weapons, we can eliminate these variables as well.

Chapters 4 and 5 examine the rise of two amalgamated security communities among traditionally hostile and competitive states. Chapter 4 an-
alyzes the integration of the Italian peninsula, a region that was historically
governed by a classic balance of power system comprised of states lacking a
common language or common culture. Chapter 5 investigates the integration of central Europe under a German federation. Like the Italian peninsula, this region had no history of close collaboration or affinity. Quite the
contrary, for centuries the principalities jealously guarded their sovereignty
and resisted attempts to create a German *Reich*.

In all three cases the development of new identities was facilitated by changes in the social structure of Europe, brought about by the French revolution and the revolutions of 1848. The cases will show that it was changing conceptions of legitimate statehood rather than a changing distribution of capabilities that most influenced the course of European history in the nineteenth century.

Methodology, Definitions, and Potential Pitfalls

Making empirical arguments about identity is, in the words of one of my reviewers, always difficult and methodologically treacherous. Social identity is an intersubjective concept that is manifested in group consciousness, rather than a material entity that can be measured by quantitative standards. It is therefore not easy to "prove" that a particular actor shares a common social identity with others. Moreover, unlike material-based variables, intersubjective ones are essentially constitutive rather than causal.[32] That is, they do not cause behavior but rather influence action by helping to define social situations and the quality of the actors with whom individuals come into contact.[33] This makes it difficult to draw a direct link between the identity of the actors and their political preferences. It is doubly difficult when dealing with historical cases, since we cannot conduct interviews or make outcome-blind predictions that would later confirm or refute the existence of a particular identity. Finally, there is the problem of measurement: how strong does an identity have to be to produce a change in attitude and behavior?

Recognizing these potential problems, we must rely on systematic observation and interpretation. Generally there are at least two ways to determine in a given case whether a group identity exists and whether this identity affects subsequent political choices. First, one can examine the nature of discourse that characterizes the interactions among specified political actors. The surest sign that a society or group has adopted a new concept or understanding is the development of a new vocabulary in terms of which the concept can then be publicly articulated.[34] Specifically, do the actors speak of themselves in terms of being part of a social group? How do they characterize others with whom they interact, both positively and negatively? Do they appear to make conceptual distinctions between groups, that is, do they speak of a special bond among specified actors? In short, the researcher looks for consistent patterns in the way the given actors define themselves, their situations, and their interaction partners.

Using the scale described below, we ask whether the content of the dis-

course is consistent with symbiosis, hostility, or any of the identities in between. This requires an analysis of internal memoranda, published historical
accounts, diplomatic exchanges, public statements, treaties, and memoirs in
order to reconstruct how the relevant actors perceived themselves, their situations, and their relationships vis-à-vis other actors.

Some writers argue that discourses and ideas are a mask covering up
deeper material interests.[35] While this may be true in some or even many
cases, it does not refute the use of discourse analysis as an indication of
attitude and belief. Discourses that are conducted in terms of a social group
identity are an explicit acknowledgment of that group's existence and, more
important, constitute a recognition that the actor wishes to be identified with
the group. That the actor is doing so to gain some material benefit presupposes that he or she sees a connection between group interest and individual
interest. At an rate, assuming that an actor's words reflect her or his true
intentions is no more presumptuous than divining what her true "deeper
interests" really are.[36]

A second method for determining the existence and constitutive power
of a given social identity is through an analysis and interpretation of individual and group *behavior*. Specifically, the researcher seeks to determine if
the specified actors behave in a manner consistent with their identities in
circumstances where they would otherwise not be expected to do so. This
approach raises the problem of causation mentioned above. How can we
know that a particular action or behavior is the result of one's identity rather
than some other variable? This is a difficult issue, even in the sociological
literature.

One way of attacking this problem is to stipulate in advance what actions
one should expect an actor to take absent a group identity, given a set of
material conditions (for example, the distribution of power, economic status,
or strategic environment). If they depart from this expected behavior, the
researcher tries to determine if their observed action is consistent with what
one should expect a member of that social group to take. In this context the
following four elements will count as evidence for a group identity and a
group consciousness: first, if the specified actors from different states act as
partners rather than adversaries or competitors in their deliberations and
interactions; second, if there is a clear concept of a group interest or common
good among the participants; third, if the state officials approach the question of European reconstruction at least partially from a discernible European and great power perspective (in the case of chapter 3) and if they
approach the strategic questions from discernible Italian and German per-

spectives (in chapters 4 and 5, respectively). Finally, if this influenced the process and outcome of the deliberations, it will count as evidence for the constitutive power of transnational identity.

The measurement question can be dealt with by treating identity as a continuum from negative to positive, ranging from conceiving the other as the social or cultural opposite of the self to viewing the other as an extension of self.[37] Building from this premise, a pure-positive social identity can be defined as *symbiosis*, a relationship in which the actors view each other as extensions of themselves. A highly positive but less intense identification can be defined as *altruism*, where the actors retain their individuality but are so closely identified with another that they are willing to make sacrifices on their behalf. The next level on the continuum is *cohesion*, a situation in which actors recognize a common good among themselves and view themselves as part of a conceptual group. The middle level is *indifference*; the actors are not important enough to each other to have any positive or negative evaluations.

A moderate form of negativity is *rivalry*; others are seen as competitors and objects for the fulfillment of self-interest. The most intense negative identification is *hostility*, a situation where the actors hold a mutual antagonism to the point of seeing each other as the "antiself" or enemy.

FIGURE 1. Measurement of Identity

Hostility	Rivalry	**Indifference**	Cohesion	Altruism	Symbiosis

← Negative Identity   Positive Identity →

The following pages will examine how different forms of identification help to determine the level of cooperation. To better understand this process, we turn to social identity theory and symbolic interaction sociology.

2 *Transnational Identities and International Politics*

Why should we study identity in international relations? Because identities provide a frame of reference from which political leaders can initiate, maintain, and structure their relationships with other states. These relationships can range from symbiosis to hostility, but embedded within them are a set of expectations concerning the nature of the actors. Structures, rules, and norms can motivate, constrain, and generate behavior, but ultimately political leaders interpret and evaluate the intentions and behaviors of other states, not abstract structures.[1] All relationships involve interaction between oneself and an other or among groups of selves and others. Thus, the way in which one defines self and other can influence the nature of the relationship. Material capabilities may provide the means for action, but identities help to define the social situation.

At the same time, while identities can be important variables in explaining behavior and interest, sometimes the nature of the actors is less important for structuring relationships than other factors such as domestic politics or the distribution of capabilities. My only claim at this point is that these are not universal factors that we can determine a priori, rather they depend upon the contexts of what symbolic interactionist sociologists call the particular social situations.[2] In some situations states act autonomously, driven by an egoistic definition of interest that is better explained by structural variables than by identity. In these cases other states are considered objects for achieving egoistic goals and relative gains concerns may be paramount. In other situations, however, states act as part of a conceptual social group and thus view the others as partners. Under these circumstances identities can help the actors define the situation by providing them with a standard for judgment and evaluation. If, as I suggested in the introduction, security arrangements can range from an international state of nature to a fully integrated amalgamated security community, then we need a theory that can explain how states can overcome the polarizing effects of anarchy and create transnational political communities.

This chapter offers such a contextual analysis by examining the relationship between identity, interest, and behavior in international relations. More specifically, it discusses the conditions under which transnational identities can transform an egoistic definition of self to one based on membership in a conceptual social group. This forms the foundation of a transnational community. It draws from social identity theory and strategic interaction models to show how the "self-other" distinctions that underlie identity helps political leaders to frame their interests and develop relationships with other states. It also shows how these definitions can change. It does so in three stages.

First, I examine the social construction of a state's *parochial* (or egoistic) identity and its effect on definitions of interest and subsequent behavior. Second, I discuss how specific forms of interaction among states can lead to the development of transnational or social identities; further, I state the conditions under which such a development is likely. Third, I demonstrate the way transnational identities can transform a state's conception of interest and its relationships with other states, arguing that in situations where transnational identities are considered more salient than parochial ones, states are likely to act as a group member rather than as an autonomous unit. This forms the basis for a transnational political community. Finally, I suggest the conditions under which this is likely to occur.

The Question of Identity in International Relations

Two literatures upon which one can draw to build a theory of identity in international relations are social identity theory (SIT), which has its roots in social psychology, and symbolic interactionist sociology (SIS), which is rooted in social theory. While these models come from different intellectual traditions, both address the social nature of the self as constituted by society.[3] Specifically, they both view human actors as differentiated into multiple identities that reside in circumscribed practices such as roles and norms. Their research is thus centered on the idea of a multifaceted and dynamic self that mediates the relationship between social structure and individual behavior. While SIT emphasizes the social group and the identification of members within the group, SIS focuses on interaction processes and the symbolic meanings that individuals assign to particular situations.

Social identity theory argues, in part, that individuals are socially constructed by the conceptual groups to which they belong.[4] It holds that actors develop conceptual ties to one another through the creation of social identities. These identities can lead to group solidarity and collective action. SIT models place the social group in the center of their investigation by emphasizing the social forces and psychological pressures that help members of social groups to differentiate themselves from other groups, for example, genders, classes, ethnicities, and political communities. This occurs through three processes: *categorization*, where individuals mentally partition the world into comprehensive units, *identification*, where actors define themselves and are viewed by others as members of certain social categories, and *social comparison* between groups, which helps actors distinguish between their conceptual "in-group" and other out-groups. SIT research seeks to explain intragroup solidarity and intergroup conflict by showing the ways in which individuals identify themselves and their interests with the group.

The application of SIT in this book runs directly counter to political scientist Jonathan Mercer's interpretation of SIT for international relations. Mercer sees SIT as *supporting* the neorealist assumption that states are a priori self-regarding, the opposite conclusion from the one offered in this chapter.[5] The primary difference can be found in how we each define the group and the prospects for redefinition. Mercer takes the autonomous state as his starting point and limits his definition of group to those living within the state's juridical borders. Thus, he uses SIT to make an argument for why states (defined as in-groups) are predisposed toward suspicion and fear in their relations with other states (out-groups). Arguing that groups are inherently competitive, he holds that "once we assume that we have two states, we can assume each will compete against the other regardless of the other's behavior."[6]

The main problem in Mercer's interpretation is that he does not allow either for group redefinitions or multiple group identities. This is illustrated by his preference for the term *other-help* rather than Alexander Wendt's *prosocial* in describing situations in which interstate relations are cohesive.[7] Other-help implies that states will naturally view all states but their own as others, and thus any cooperative gestures will either be self-interested or altruistic. However, individuals and corporate actors usually belong to many in-groups, some of which overlap and some of which conflict. One can simultaneously be French, European, and Catholic. It is theoretically unjustified to automatically assume that all group memberships will conflict, apart from the particular situation and the particular groups involved. Indeed, SIT views the group as developing *within* society, in this case international society, and clearly rebuffs the notion that the self (the sovereign state) is either independent from or existing prior to society.

Moreover, the logic of his argument implies that state boundaries are static and unchanging. Yet one of his own examples, ethnocentrism, demonstrates the limits of focusing only on ingroup behavior. Ethnocentrism is indeed a powerful barrier to the formation of transnational identities, yet throughout modern history societies and cultures have often redefined their nationality by moving either to higher levels of aggregation (political integration) or to lower ones (secession). This suggests that identities are dynamic and that sovereignty is not an impenetrable barrier to transnational community building.

SIT's emphasis on group behavior and group processes can thus help us to understand how individuals can act within the context of a conceptual social group, for example as Arabs as well as Egyptians. Symbolic interactionist sociology can augment this through its emphasis on the dynamics of social interaction and how this can influence the construction and reconstruction of roles.

Symbolic interaction theories hold that the "self" is always in the process of *being* (reproducing) and *becoming* (changing). The main premise of SIS is that human beings do not typically respond directly to stimuli but rather assign meanings to the stimuli and act on the basis of these meanings. SIS thus focuses primarily on the way actors create, interpret, and define (or redefine) social situations through the use of symbols, framing, and role making.[8] These situations are defined and interpreted by the participants, who act toward each other on the basis of their intersubjective definitions. Thus, actors assign meaning to acts, objects, and individuals in terms of their joint relationship to the situation.[9] Identities and the social roles that are derived from them influence the way meaning is assigned and therefore influence behavior. Action, then, is influenced by social interaction and definitions of the present situation.[10]

In the following pages I will integrate these two approaches into a model that explains how transnational identities can shift the conceptual boundaries that divide states. The application of these models to international relations theory requires a conceptual move from the individual/societal level to that of the state/interstate environment. This requires two conditions: first, a theory of agency that allows us to treat states as coherent social actors with definable identities and second, a theory that shows how states collectively comprise a society through which sociological factors can operate.

Most neorealists would deny that the international environment can be considered a society, and thus social theories would not be applicable to international relations. Following Hobbes, neorealism tends to view society in terms of a legal social order that can only function with the construction of a central authority that will "keep everyone in awe." Lacking a Leviathan with the power and authority to make laws, adjudicate disputes, and enforce rules, a functional international society cannot develop.[11]

Neither the SIS nor SIT models, however, require the existence of either a central authority or a single value system that is accepted by all members of society. Sociologists study relationships among individuals and groups that occur in a social context regardless of how or even whether they are formally governed. Symbolic interactionist Sheldon Stryker, for example, simply defines society as "patterned, organized interaction," while SIT proponents Hogg and Abrams see society as comprising large-scale social categories that stand in power and status relations to one another.[12] In both models society is conceptualized not as a static external force influencing or determining behavior but as an interaction process.

While these models would not be applicable in an international state of nature where communication and interaction are minimal or even nonexistent, they are clearly consistent with Hedley Bull's "Anarchical Society."[13] Thus, we can build a model of transnational identity *without* assuming that the international environment itself would need to transform from a self-help system (as defined by Waltz) to a prosocial one.[14]

The next condition for applying these sociological models to the international system requires a reasonable assumption that states can behave as social actors with definable identities in their relations with one other. This is not to deny differences between individual and corporate actors, rather it simply means that the processes that facilitate identity formation and human social behavior are similar at different levels of aggregation. We need to assume that states (through their agents) can interact, categorize, form relationships, interpret behavior, and exchange signals with other states. There are in general three approaches to suggest that enduring environmental forces produce a constancy of state action that justifies attributing identities, interests, and roles to states: first, to equate the state with its top officials or government, second, to treat the state as an institutional actor, where state officials express the continuity of its institutions, and third, to portray the state as a corporate entity with stable identities, thus attributing to the state a national personality or collective consciousness.[15]

For the purposes of this study I favor a combination of the first and second approaches. States can be understood as integrated sets of political institutions that hold supreme authority within internationally recognized territories.[16] They reflect the histories, geographies, cultures, social institutions, and class structures of the societies over which they rule, but they also have an independent existence. In this sense states act more like "trustees" than "servants" of their societies. While we can assume that they reflect the dominant domestic political actors, they also act with a fair amount of autonomy in promoting the goals of society.[17] Under normal circumstances the institutional structure of the state remains relatively constant regardless of who controls the mechanisms of government.[18] This tends to change only after a social revolution or radical regime transformation. As a result, the institutions of the state possess a high level of continuity, coherence, and stability that allows for state agency.

The balance of domestic political forces is reflected in the composition of the ruling coalition, which represents the dominant social groups in society.[19] As long as the ruling coalition remains in control of the state, there should be relative stability in its institutional structure. Thus, while state leaders are the agents of action, they are embedded in an institutional structure that provides for a form of socialization and coherence across time and domain so long as the regime type (or form of state) remains constant.[20] This allows for the emergence and maintenance of relatively stable identities.

Moreover, states themselves can attain the status of political actor in international affairs by virtue of their relationship with other states. Theda Skocpol argues: "The linkage of states into transnational structures and into international flows of communication may encourage leading state officials to pursue transformative strategies even in the face of indifference or resistance from politically weighty social forces."[21] Consequently, when I use the term *state* in this book I am referring to a stable institutional structure that is represented by its political leadership. For this reason the empirical chapters will focus on the interaction among state elites. For the purpose of evaluating the evidence, a common identity among the sovereigns, ministers, and revolutionary leaders from different states will be viewed as synonymous with a transnational identity.

State Identities and the Definition of Self

The study of identity in international relations involves at least two components: conceptions of self and other held uniquely by each state (state identity) and self-other conceptions that encompass broader social categories that are shared by at least two states (transnational identity). Intuitively, we may be tempted to simply divide them by assuming that state identities are determined by domestic politics and that transnational identities are created through interaction among state officials on the international stage. Indeed, identity theories suggest such a dichotomy by arguing that all actors have both personal identities—a conception of oneself as unique and distinct from others—and social identities—that part of the self-concept that is derived from the social category to which one is associated.[22] However, the most interesting sociological and social-psychological work on understanding the self and its relationship to the other suggests a more complex model.

Parochial identities are rooted in a consciousness of difference; they emerge from an individual's understanding of oneself as being in many ways unique. However, on one level even parochial identities can be considered to be social/interactive in character because for one to consider oneself to be distinct, she must have some conception of what she is distinct from. This is an inherently social process in which "I and thou" are mutually constituted. This dialectic is the basis of what George Herbert Mead refers to as the "self."[23] Similarly, while domestic politics and national culture clearly play an important role in facilitating a national identity, they are mediated by the participation of the state in international society.

Mead argues that the self arises through social experience. Once it has arisen, it continues to be defined and redefined through the process of interaction.[24] This point is key, because the concept of a self is the basic ingredient for an identity, whether we are talking about an individual or a corporate actor. Unlike biological models, which classify organisms according to their essential characteristics such as physiological attributes, human identities are not inborn, nor can they exist apart from one's relations with others. If individuals were socially autonomous from society, there would be no need to consider one's identity. A Robinson Crusoe, for example, has no basis from which to develop a concept of self, since he has no standard of comparison. One can make a Hegelian claim that he is conscious, but not *self*-conscious, because this requires the presence of an other.[25] As soon as he comes into contact with another, however, his egoistic understanding of himself would inevitably be challenged, and he would be forced to locate his individuality within a social context.

Sociologists speak of identities in terms of "social locations" relative to the various individuals and social categories with whom actors come into contact.[26] They are defined in terms of self and other that arise in the process of social experience and activity.[27] This is because it is only through our interaction with others that we become conscious of our similarities and differences. As Hegel points out, to be conscious of oneself as a unit implies distinguishing between one's self and those determinate characteristics that differentiate one from other people. To be conscious of what one is, is to be conscious of what one is not.[28] One's ethnicity, for example, only becomes apparent when one comes in contact with other ethnic groups; ethnicity is not a defining characteristic in a uni-ethnic society. This contact could either render one's ethnic characteristics important or irrelevant, depending upon the nature of the interaction.[29] Race is an important characteristic only in a race-conscious society. Brown-eyed people, for example, do not generally view their eye color as socially significant, nor do they attribute any particular set of expectations or assumptions about other brown-eyed people.

Symbolic interactionist theories hold that actors have many selves, with each related to the interactions with which he or she is involved.[30] Thus, each person is a unique combination of various characteristics and social locations. As we interact with others, we become aware of ourselves as objects (as well as subjects) and come to see, assess, judge, and create identities. This combination of our various selves constitutes our parochial identity. The significance of one's identity for understanding behavior often depends upon the particular social situation. People often know what to expect of each other in particular situations because they know that various types of people behave in typical ways under particular circumstances.[31] For example, as a daughter, one may behave in a certain manner vis-à-vis one's parents, while the daughter may see herself (and act) entirely differently in a situation where she is defined as an employer. Thus, identities are "situated" within specific contexts. For this reason, Mead argues that the self is complex and differentiated. Once the self arises, it continues to be defined and redefined through interaction.

As we move from one situated identity to another we develop a cumulative sense of the others who are important to us, either positively or negatively. Sociologists refer to these as "reference others" or, if they comprise conceptual categories, "reference groups."[32] Reference others help individuals to form judgments about themselves by serving as points of comparison or standards of judgment, thus facilitating the process of self-definition and ultimately identity formation. Both individual and institutional actors continually compare themselves to others, positively and negatively, in part to better define who they are and, equally important, who they are not. Thus even parochial identities are socially constructed, owing much to the nature of one's relations and interactions with (or against) others. While all individuals are motivated by certain innate drives and needs—for example, hunger, sleep, and personal security—it is impossible to understand one's *interests* in a social environment apart from knowing their situated identity. For rational choice to operate one must be able to deduce a set of ordered goals from the actors. This means either to assume a fixed set of interests such as power maximization (as Morganthau does) or to try to determine what kinds of actors pursue what kinds of goals in what kinds of situations.

While states are obviously more complex than individuals, they too have definable personalities and identities that serve to distinguish them from other states. Like the case of individuals in society, state identities are also formed in large part through a process of social interaction and social comparison, and this in turn affects conceptions of self. A state that has had no contact with other states cannot have an identity, since there would be no standard of comparison or location of self. Because all states have a particular history and represent a unique combination of domestic institutions and cultural practices, no two states can have the same parochial identity. The institution of sovereignty enables a state to develop its own unique personality, which provides the material basis for the construction of a "self." Yet sovereignty is itself dependent upon a process of differentiation and self-categorization that can only exist within a broader social environment. In fact a political community cannot even be considered a state unless it participates in the nation-state system; states exist as "sovereign" entities by virtue of their independence from other states.

As Anthony Giddens suggests, the sovereignty of the nation-state does not precede the development of the state system. That is, state authorities were not originally empowered with an absolute sovereignty, destined to become confined by a growing network of international connections. Rather, the development of state sovereignty depended—and still depends—upon a monitored set of relations between states. " 'International relations' are not connections set up between pre-established states," Giddens argues, "which could maintain their sovereignty without them: they are the basis upon which nation-states exist at all."[33]

Thus, even on its most basic level, the sovereign state develops its identity as a state through its associations within the nation-state system, and its unique consciousness is formed by differentiation from other states. France exists as an independent sovereign entity with its own national personality and identity through its distinction from Spain, Germany, and so on. The identity of being French provides a rationale for developing a particularly "French interest," rather than a European or Catholic one for example, but only because of the existence of non-French states. Through its interaction and communication with other states, its agents categorize, compare themselves to, and occasionally try to emulate them. Its agents became self-conscious, and this affects both the meaning and future development of its institutions. If the French are perceived as quirky and fiercely independent in their relations with other states (including their allies), it is only because we have developed a standard for state behavior by comparing them to other states.

In an international society of states, then, state identities are largely constituted through their relationships with other states. States achieve an understanding of "self" through the process of social comparison and categorization. One cannot deduce identities apart from the historical context through which this interaction occurs. As with the case of individuals, a particular characteristic of a society can either be rendered significant or irrelevant depending upon the context. For example, religious and dynastic identities were the most salient characteristics in defining self and interest within the European state system for much of the sixteenth and seventeenth centuries.[34] One did not speak of the "Austrians" as much as one did of the "Hapsburgs." Austrian interests were synonymous with dynastic interests and, in some contexts, Catholic interests. With the rise of nationalism, however, both religious and dynastic identities were downplayed in favor of cultural or ethnic attributes. Similarly, when independent states amalgamate into a single entity—such as Italy or Germany in the nineteenth century—or break apart into smaller entities—such as the former Soviet Union or Yugoslavia—there is a clear change in the characteristics that are considered most salient in defining the self as a corporate entity.

"National" identity—and following from this, national loyalty—are thus products of differentiation among societies. The construction of a national identity is achieved through the creation of conceptual boundaries that separate the domestic (the self) from the foreign (the other). These boundaries are not natural formations, and they often change over time. However, the way in which political actors draw them greatly influences the way in which the state and its population distinguishes itself and its interests in international society. A narrowly conceived nationalism, for example, places a clear boundary between one's ethnic or civic community and all others.[35] Broader attachments are considered less important or even detrimental, and interests tend to be defined in highly parochial terms. Yet a more broadly conceived transnationalism can extend the definition of one's community to include populations from other societies, for example, pan-Slavism or pan-Arabism.

It depends upon how one defines "the nation," and this has important consequences for definitions of interest and for the legitimation of, for example, a separate Arab state apart from the broader Arab nation. At the same time, a broadly conceived cosmopolitanism, for example, Europeanism, extends the definition of self to include a far broader conceptual category of people and societies than does ethnic nationalism. While political actors and populations having such an identity retain attachments to their own political communities, they also identify themselves and their interests with those of a broader group that crosses political borders.

The concept of patriotism as loyalty to one's own country presupposes a conceptual tie between the population, or at least the political elites, and the state. This tie is presumed to be greater than other bonds, such as religion, ethnicity, and regionalism. The institution of sovereignty provides the material foundation for this bond; however, this is by no mean static or unalterable. Since national identities, like other types of group consciousness, are constructed, they are capable of being reconstructed or transformed. T. A. Elliot demonstrates, for example, how racial identities in Africa became reclassified as national when they became attached to a particular territory after decolonization.[36] This was also the prerequisite for the creation of the Italian and German nations in the mid-nineteenth century.

Historical factors can have an important impact on a political unit's conception of "self" and the degree to which this definition of self is based on political, ethnic, social, or geographic characteristics. The modern state formed long before nationalism provided it with an identity based on the composition of the population.[37] The formation of most territorial states in Europe preceded the development of the modern conception of the nation, which did not arise in most of Europe until after the French revolution.[38] The state in the early modern period had no particular identity apart from the king's lineage until it became differentiated from other states. The fusion of crown and state created political units based on personal loyalty to the king or prince, but it would be stretching the meaning of the terms to say that there was a "national identity" or "national interest" beyond the perceived preferences of the monarchy. Identity and interest were not necessarily tied to a specific territory; political boundaries were fluid, and many territories changed hands frequently. Thus even geography was not a stable foundation for identity or interest.

In contemporary international society the creation and re-creation of conceptual boundaries continues to play a vital role in the development and transformation of identities and interests. Some of the variance in a state's identity can be explained by domestic politics. For example, the change in

Iran's identity in 1979 from a Persian to a Shiite Muslim state was the result of social revolution and a change in regime. The emergence of a radically different ruling coalition laid the foundation for this change. However, to the extent that identities are built and maintained through evaluative comparisons between in-groups (the self) and relevant out-groups (the other), domestic politics is intricately tied to the international environment. Iran's "Islamic revolution" (to the extent that it was such) was defined in part by its opposition to the West (the other) and its solidarity with Islam (a transnational political force).[39] The reference group or society that provided the standard for social comparison was the United States and other "Western" nations, which many Iranians blamed for contributing toward their oppression. In this case new identities were created from a negative comparative process. Later Iran itself became a reference group, albeit a positive one, for other political actors within other countries seeking to create Islamic states, for example Afghanistan.

Like the complex and differentiated self that comprises the individual, states represent a variety of societal institutions and practices that gain social meaning when they are contrasted with other types of institutions and practices. Thus states have many identities, each of which is situated within a specific context. These situated identities enable states to occupy different social positions or roles in different situations. For example, in the late nineteenth century, Great Britain could act (and be generally viewed by others) as the "mother of all parliaments" in its relations with emerging democracies in Europe and North America while at the same time imposing itself as a colonial bully in its relations with India.

In fact, Britain was both a democracy and an empire, which made for a complex and differentiated national personality. One might argue that its identity as the first modern European democracy contradicted its role as a colonial empire, however, the creation of different social situations enabled Britain to act differently in various contexts without undermining its legitimacy or identity. The self-serving conceptual distinction between civilized and uncivilized—a transnational distinction—enabled Britain to justify this seemingly contradictory behavior to its population and European neighbors.[40]

Identities can affect interest not only by providing a standard of comparison and expectation but also by influencing one's choice of reference groups and the degree to which these groups are viewed positively or negatively. Returning to a previous example, prior to 1979 Iran considered itself to be a modern westernizing state within a region of hostile cultures (its population is Persian, not Arab). As such, its ruling coalition saw the United States as its key superpower ally. Following its revolution in 1979, Iran identified itself as an Islamic state, which formed the basis of its relations with other states. Its traditional ally became the "Great Satan" and its main competitor for regional hegemony, Syria, became an ally. Moreover, Iran so strongly identified with its role as leader of the Islamic world that it deliberately alienated both superpowers simultaneously, a move that cannot be explained by classical balance of power theory.

Transnational Identities and the Construction of a Social Group

Up to this point I have focused primarily on the way states distinguish themselves from other states and how this can affect their relationships with and behavior toward each other. I argued that a state's parochial identity is formed through a process of conceptual differentiation between domestic and foreign, or self and other. These identities are reinforced by the institution of sovereignty, which legitimizes political distinctions based on geography and nationality. Thus, states are predisposed to favor their parochial identities. However, states do not exist in isolation from each other but are rather connected in a complex network of relationships—both positive and negative—that provide opportunities for creating, strengthening, or weakening their identifications with each other.

If state identities are formed and reinforced through social comparison and categorization, it follows that they can also be transformed and expanded through this same process. While communication, comparison, and interaction among political actors can uncover difference and distinctiveness, they can also lead to a consciousness of commonality that moves or even erases the conceptual boundaries between states.

Hogg and Abrams argue that there is a continuum of self-conception ranging from exclusively social to exclusively personal identity and that when social identities become more salient than personal identities the resulting behavior is qualitatively different.[41] The determination of which identity will inform a state's interest—and thereby influence its subsequent behavior—depends upon *identity salience*, that is, the relative importance of one particular identity in relation to others in a particular situation.[42] If one has several conflicting identities, the relative location of one particular identity on the "salience hierarchy" becomes an important predictor of behavior. When the salience of one's social identity is high, group interests become synonymous with state interests, because the actors perceive that their fortunes are tied to those of the group.

It is difficult to determine what the identity salience of a state will be at a particular time, apart from the domestic and international circumstances that exist. Stryker, however, argues that identity salience can be determined by the degree to which an actor is committed to a particular set of relationships. Thus, a state may act against its parochial instincts if its leadership believes that such behavior is necessary to maintain good relations with those whom they value. For example, the United States may act against its own domestic constituents in economic affairs in cases where the cohesiveness of the Group of Seven is at stake. In this instance it would be acting to enhance its role as an economic leader of advanced capitalist states at the expense of domestic politics.

States, like individuals, belong to a variety of social as well as parochial categories. Individuals are not only defined by their personal characteristics but by their group qualities, such as ethnicity, class, gender, religion, and profession. And, like individuals, states not only represent societies defined by their internal qualities—culture, history, geography, political institutions—but also by their association with broader conceptual social groups that transcend juridical borders.[43] These groups together furnish states with a repertoire of discrete category memberships (social identities) that help to define them in their relations with other states. The mutual recognition by particular states that these social categories are part of their self-concepts, as well as their knowledge that they belong to certain social groups, forms the basis for transnational identities.

Like transnational communities, transnational identities—social identities that transcend juridical borders—can form either among societal groups or among states. Like all types of collective identities, they express a change in the level of abstraction of self-categorization, that is, a shift from a definition of self as unique and distinct to one that perceives the self as an part of a conceptual social category or group that transcends state boundaries. Put another way, they express a change in the way states make self-other distinctions. Social identity theory holds that a transformation of identities can occur when actors develop conceptual attachments to selective others through the processes of recategorization, recomparison, and reidentification. When a group of states recognize that they share a common set of social characteristics and experiences that define them as a unique group in distinction from other conceptual groups, they have created a transnational identity. I argue that transnational identity formation requires both material and intersubjective conditions. At a minimum, the necessary material conditions include the following:

First, there must be a *shared characteristic* that can form the material basis for a transnational social group, such as a common ethnicity, region, form of state, political or economic system, or relative level of development. The more salient this characteristic is to a society's self-understanding, the more likely it is to value its transnational attachments with those sharing the attribute. For example, both England and Germany are European states, however, it has been apparent over the past few decades that Germany values its ties to Europe and the European ideal more than England does.

Second, there must be a shared *exclusive relationship* to the other states in the system or region. Exclusivity is key to group cohesion and helps to highlight the distinctions between those sharing a common social characteristic and those who do not. In short, exclusive relationships highlight a self-other distinction by creating positive and negative reference groups.

For example, for many years, the relations among democratic states were conducted on a different basis (reflecting different expectations) than those between democracies and nondemocracies.[44] The exclusiveness of their relationships was facilitated in part by their minority status in a world dominated by autocratic regimes. Over time this created a unique set of norms that guided their behavior toward each other, which was not generally extended to autocracies. The division of Europe between liberal democracies and communist bureaucracies after World War II both reflected and solidified this relationship.

Third, there must be a high level of *positive interdependence* between the states. Interdependence lowers the conceptual boundaries that are created by juridical borders, and this can help to lead to a broader definition of "self" that moves beyond territorial distinctions. The interdependence must be *positive*—that is, mutually rewarding—otherwise it could lead to resentment and conflict.[45] When a group of actors depend upon each other to satisfy at least one of their primary needs and achieve satisfaction from their association, they tend to develop feelings of mutual attraction that strengthens the group.[46] Interdependence can vary in duration, reward level, and intensity, and these three variables determine the degree to which an interdependent relationship will contribute toward a transnational identity. I argue that *the greater the degree of interdependence and the higher the reward level, the stronger the social attachments and the greater the potential for transnational identity formation.*

While these three material conditions can provide a foundation for the development of a common identity, they cannot in and of themselves *create* this identity. Social identities are intersubjective phenomena and thus have no practical expression apart from their recognition by the actors involved.

Lacking a political consciousness, objective conditions will not necessarily translate into intersubjective understandings. For example, although European states have long shared a common geographic and cultural characteristic, a common relationship to non-Europeans (particularly during the colonial era) and a clear economic and social interdependence, European identities have waxed and waned over the past several hundred years. This is because European leaders have often not thought of themselves as Europeans but rather as Austrians, Hapsburgs, or Catholics. A political consciousness allows the actors to interpret the already existing material conditions in ways that make them salient to their definition of self and other.

If, as constructivists argue, there is a causal relationship between what actors do and what they are, transnational identities develop in the course of sustained interaction.[47] Since interactions can be either positive or negative, we are looking for a set of practices that demonstrate commonality. For this reason, I would argue that group identities develop out of common experiences; political actors must *act* together as a group before they can recognize the *existence* of that group. Common experiences highlight the uniqueness of a group, particularly when they are of high intensity and long duration. This is why, for example, concert systems tend to form in the aftermath of a major war.[48] The great powers recognize their special role in defeating the revisionist power and this can extend to peacetime systems management. Similarly, the development of a transnational "Third World" identity among former colonies is a good example of how a shared experience that was both highly intense and long in duration—colonialism— could facilitate the creation of a social group.

I hypothesize that *the greater the intensity and the longer the duration of the experience, the stronger the social attachments and the more likely that transnational identity will form.* Under these conditions sustained interactions can become institutionalized over time. By this I mean that the actors develop a set of practices and norms to facilitate their continued interaction. To the extent that the participants view their relationship as distinct and exclusive, these practices become attached to their group identities. In this sense, the actors socialize each other.

Transnational Identities and Behavioral Effects

Transnational identities can alter the social environment through which a group of states relate to each other by creating what Mead would call a community of attitudes or "generalized other." These communities develop particular frameworks that inform the members of the appropriate ways of responding to a situation.[49] Thus, the generalized other provides the criteria for self-assessment, reflection, signaling, and interpreting the signals of others. In Meadian terms, states sharing a transnational identity often assume the organized social attitudes of their group (or community) toward the social problems that confront them at any given time. This can generate certain types of behavior in several ways:

First, transnational identities provide the members of a social group with a set of norms, boundaries, goals, and a social context for interaction. Social identities carry with them a certain range of prerogatives and obligations an actor who is accorded that identity may carry out.[50] These prerogatives and obligations constitute the role-prescriptions associated with that identity. In any particular situation actors participate in a network of roles that define it.[51] Roles link transnational identities with action by defining the types of behaviors that are characteristic of a category of actors within a specific context. In other words, while a transnational identity defines states' social location relative to other states, the roles that are derived from these identities create expectations and assumptions about what this particular category of actors typically does in a particular situation. State elites then often exhibit a national role conception, which signals the actions that are appropriate to their state and the actions it should undertake with the international system.[52]

States sharing a transnational identity act in the context of organized patterns by recognizing each other as occupants of these roles. Actors tend to adhere to their roles when a positive relationship to its reference others depends on its being a particular type of actor. Under these circumstances its ability to maintain a positive transnational identity, as well as its "membership" in the transnational social group, is tied to willingness to act in a certain manner. For example, democratic states are expected to conduct their foreign relations according to the "rule of law," at least in their dealings with each other, and the community of democratic states often pressures its members to do so.[53]

This is, of course, subject to interpretation and manipulation by the states inhabiting these roles. Roles proscribe a *range* of behaviors that are consistent with a particular identity. Thus, there is often conflict and/or disagreement as to what a particular identity entails, for example, what it means to "act like a great power" or "act like a European." However there are limits to how far a state can deviate from accepted group norms and still be considered part of the group.

At the same time, because states belong to many conceptual social groups, they have many identities, often pulling them in conflicting directions. As a result, social actors often exhibit role conflict when there are contrary expectations attached to some position in a social relationship. Such expectations could call for incompatible performances. Giddens describes this as "role strain," which manifests itself in at least two points of tension: first, between the needs and wants of the actors and the role-prescriptions that are associated with their various identities (egoistic impulses verses group norms) and second, between the role-prescriptions of different social identities that an individual is ascribed with, adopts, or is forced to assume.[54] Under these conditions a state's *situated identity* (that is, the identity that most appropriately fits the particular situation) becomes the important variable in predicting behavior. This type of contextual analysis can explain why a state may act differently in otherwise similar conditions, for example, why security dilemmas arise among some states and not others.

Second, common identities can facilitate cooperation among members of a transnational social group. Social groups exhibit a high degree of closure in the sense that the participants recognize a common membership in an organized unit and a sense of interdependency with respect to common goals.[55] States sharing a common transnational identity tend to value their associations with each other. Stryker refers to this as "commitment," which can vary in intensity from minimal to high. States that are highly committed to maintaining their relationships with certain types of states are more likely to be risk acceptant and accommodating to them, and as a group they are more likely to practice diffuse reciprocity. Thus, the higher the commitment, the greater the degree of cooperation. Moreover, states that hold a particular attribute to be highly important, for example, democracy, often find it beneficial to support others having the same attribute. Under these conditions states are less likely to worry about relative gains *within* the group than they are *between* their in-groups and other out-groups. This can promote trust and help to overcome collective action problems.

I therefore suggest that *the more a state is committed to maintaining a particular set of interstate relationships, the higher the salience of its transnational identity relative to other identities, and the more likely it will act as a member of that social group in international affairs according to group norms.* In practical terms, this means that higher levels of commitment should lead to stronger transnational identities and greater group cohesion.

Third, transnational identities can help to legitimize a particular form of state or governance structure, and, therefore, under conditions of domestic uncertainty states are more likely to act in a manner consistent with these identities. In every society there are a variety of domestic forces promoting alternative ideologies. The ruling coalition simply represents the dominant one. Transnational identities help to validate particular forms of governance or state over others by creating positive reference groups from which political actors can draw legitimacy. Reference groups help a regime or ruling coalition to justify its form of governance to its society by providing a positive standard from which domestic actors can evaluate its worthiness to rule. To the degree that the regimes can positively identify themselves with a transnational social group, they empower those domestic forces sharing that transnational identity.

This is particularly important during rapid periods of change, when social forces are in potential or actual conflict.[56] Under conditions such as these—that is, when the legitimacy of the form of state or governance is seriously challenged either domestically or internationally—states are more likely to act in a manner consistent with their transnational identity. To fail to do so could undermine their position vis-à-vis competing groups. Moreover, domestic political actors are often more concerned with protecting transnational values than those associated with the doctrine of *raison d'état*, for example, pan-nationalism, monarchy, or republicanism. A state that fails to reflect these values loses support and legitimacy.

Michael Barnett demonstrates, for example, that Arab governments were often highly constrained in their ability to promote a purely parochial state interest at the expense of the greater Arab nation.[57] Such behavior would undermine their legitimacy as an Arab state, thereby threatening their domestic support among the population. Internationally, a gap between a transnational identity and a state's expected behavior could undermine its legitimacy vis-à-vis the other members of the transnational social group sharing that same identity. This could result in the exclusion of that state from the very community in which it hoped to participate. This places limits on the degree to which a state can promote a policy of raison d'état if this policy appears to violate the norms of the transnational social group.

Fourth, transnational identities are often institutionalized within international associations that help to socialize their members according to group norms. To be a member of any group is to accept the norms associated with membership. To the degree that the association is taken as a positive reference group, the participants take on the roles associated with them. The exclusive nature of these associations helps to highlight the self-other distinction that forms the basis of an identity. Conceptions of self are often linked to ideal conceptions of what one ought to be, which are linked both to group membership and an us-them distinction between social groups.

These exclusive associations help to highlight and strengthen the transnational identities they embody. Thus states become more "European" by participating in the European Union, more "Third World" by their membership in the Group of Seventy-Seven, and more "Arab" by their participation in the Arab League. To the extent that this is viewed as beneficial for the states involved, the social group grows stronger. Thus, *the greater the perceived benefits of group membership, the stronger the identity, and the more likely each state will act as a member of the group.*

Transnational Identities and Transnational Communities

In chapter 1 I defined a transnational political community as a collectivity of political actors organized on the basis of common values and a common good that transcends juridical borders. Such communities act with at least some degree of internal consensus in their relations with outside states. The development of transnational identities enables states to construct such communities by diminishing the conceptual and political boundaries that separate them. Under the conditions cited above transnational identities can transform egoistic conceptions of self to perceptions of commonality by creating a community of attitudes or generalized other. This does not mean that conflicts cease among members of the community. Indeed, disagreements over the proper roles and norms members are expected to assume or follow can be intense.

Moreover, other factors, principally sovereignty and anarchy, continue to exert pressures *against* group cohesion. What distinguishes the dynamics of transnational community from other relationships or forms of cooperation, however, is that the members generally hold a concept of a common good, not simply common interests. Transnational communities are sustained through a commitment by their members to maintaining a particular set of social relationships with each other. The type of community is determined by the type of transnational identity.

Transnational identities do not develop easily and transnational security communities are hard to construct. The polarizing effects of sovereignty and anarchy are formidable obstacles. Thus, transnational communities are most likely to form during and following periods of social upheaval, when domestic institutions are challenged, international orders are undermined, and traditional structures are eroded. During these periods contending political actors often seek new forms of legitimation, allowing, for a brief period, a redefinition of political boundaries. Sometimes state actors respond by looking inward and increase their parochialism, as was done in Germany and Italy during the interwar period. At other times political actors reevaluate their parochialism and discover new foundations for commonality, as the cases in the next three chapters demonstrate. These periods of reflection and reidentification offer the greatest possibilities for overcoming the barriers of anarchy.

The next section will closely examine three cases in which state leaders constructed cohesive security arrangements on the basis of a transnational identity. To the extent that the cases illustrate the points argued above, they offer evidence of the power of transnational identity in international relations.

Part 2

*Transnational Community in
Nineteenth-Century Europe*

3 A Great Power Concert and a Community of Monarchs

International relations scholars often cite European diplomatic history as offering the strongest evidence for balance of power theory in practice. Between the shifting alliance patterns, imperial competition, continental wars, and ongoing bids for hegemonic dominance, the flow of European history appears to confirm the proposition that conflict and rivalry is the inevitable outcome of political relations in an anarchical environment.

Yet European history also shows evidence of political leaders trying to overcome these conditions. From 1815 to approximately 1854, Europe was governed by two parallel systems of collective management. The first consisted of five mutually acknowledged "great powers" who acted as trustees for European security. This system has been alternatively referred to as the European pentarchy, the confederation of Europe, the Vienna system, and the Concert of Europe. The second was a common security association of Eastern monarchies whose purpose was to uphold the interests of an aristocratic, European social order through maintaining the 1815 Settlement by means of a repressive alliance of monarchical states.[1] This has been informally labeled the Metternich system and the Holy Alliance. In both cases the balance of power was replaced by a community of power.

While the practice of consultation and collaboration that defined these systems waxed and waned, they remained cohesive for approximately four decades.[2] This presents us with a historical puzzle that cannot be explained by structural theories. The conditions leading up to the Congress of Vienna in 1815 clearly favored the development of a competitive balance of power system, particularly in central Europe. Austria and Prussia were traditional rivals, aggravated by the fact that they bordered each other and had conflicting territorial claims.[3] In fact, much of eighteenth century diplomacy focused on the growing rivalry between Austria (the Hapsburg Empire) and Prussia for the domination of the Holy Roman Empire, leading to several major wars. The introduction of Russia into the European political scene only complicated matters. Russia's expansion southward and westward challenged the Hapsburg's position as the dominant political force in central Europe.

Coming out of the Napoleonic wars, Britain and Austria had seen the possible expansion of Russian power as the biggest potential security problem that Europe would face after the defeat of France.[4] During this period it was common for European leaders to predict that Russia, by virtue of its size, population, and geographic advantage, would succeed Napoleonic France as the dominant power on the continent, competing with Britain for supremacy.[5] While the war against France provided a temporary unifying cause for the European powers, the reintegration of France into the European system ended the wartime alliance, and therefore traditional patterns of territorial competition should have reemerged. Thus the Concert of Europe and the Holy Alliance are "hard cases" for theories of transnational identity since there were so many factors working *against* group cohesion and great power unity.[6]

While balance of power theory can explain why Britain, Austria, Prussia, and Russia would temporarily cast aside their rivalries to join the Quadruple Alliance against Napoleon, it cannot explain why this close collaboration persisted long after France was defeated. Political scientists have traditionally attributed this phenomenon to three primary causes: war weariness, strategies of reciprocity, and ideological similarity. Robert Jervis argues that concert systems form after, and only after, a large war against a potential hegemon because such a conflict produces significant ties between the allies, undermines the acceptability of war as a tool of statecraft, and, perhaps most important, increases the incentives to cooperate.[7] Applying a game theory approach, Jervis argues that changes in the payoff structure to favor cooperation and differences in the potential gains from cooperation help to explain the concert.[8] Simply put, there was an increase in gains from cooperation and a decrease in gains from exploitation. In cooperation theory terms, the explanatory variables are tit-for-tat strategies of reciprocity and an increase in the shadow of the future.[9]

Tit-for-tat strategies might be able to account for the ability of the great powers to overcome mistrust and collective action problems, however, co-operation theories do not explain why the great powers would wish to pool their resources to facilitate collective management in the first place. Equally important, there is little evidence that states actually pursued tit-for-tat strat-egies during this period. In addition, explanations based on the idea of war weariness cannot explain why a concert system evolved in 1815 but not after previous and subsequent wars when aversion to conflict was equally strong. There have been at least four major continental or world wars and numerous other smaller but widespread conflicts since the Peace of Westphalia, yet only after the Napoleonic Wars did an effective concert system develop. While the Napoleonic wars continued for a relatively long time (twenty-five years), they did not last as long as the Thirty Years War in the seventeenth century, nor were they as destructive as either World War I or II.

Some political scientists argue that the concert was the result of ideo-logical similarities between the great powers, who shared not only a common political ideology but also a common vision of the international order.[10] These factors were certainly important in creating a foundation for group cohesion. However, ideological compatibility can explain the Holy Alliance better than it can the concert, since it was precisely ideological issues that ultimately divided the Eastern from the Western great powers. While the concert focused on the management of continental security affairs, it was a common security association, the Holy Alliance, that embodied ideological solidarity by defending and restoring monarchy against domestic rebels. At the same time, even if ideological compatibility provided the necessary con-dition to explain the Holy Alliance, it does not offer a sufficient one. After the Peace of Utrich in 1714, the major powers were also all monarchies. However they did not view monarchy as a distinguishing characteristic in their definition of themselves and their neighbors. It was not until other alternatives become conceivable, principally nationalism and liberalism, that they were able to see themselves as a unique and exclusive group.

Consequently, while structural variables can account for the plurality of great powers that is necessary for a concert or common security system to form, it cannot account for their cohesion as a social group. This chapter will try to explain how and why these groups evolved.

The French Revolution as a Permissive Condition

The rise of cohesive security arrangements in nineteenth-century Europe occurred within the context of enormous social and political changes that swept the continent. Historian Paul Schreoder argues that European politics was transformed between 1763 and 1848, characterized by a fundamental change in the governing rules, norms, and practices of international relations.[11] Most scholars studying nineteenth-century European politics focus on the Napoleonic wars as the great event that altered relations among states.[12] For neorealism, in particular, war is the principal catalyst of change. This is because variations in the rules are derived from the variance in the distribution of capabilities and war is the primary means for determining relative power.[13] Thus, to the extent that the Napoleonic wars changed the balance of power in Europe and encouraged the victorious states to become status quo powers, we should be able to find a direct link between the new distribution of power and preferences for more cohesive security arrangements.

An alternative explanation, which I present in this chapter, is that the change in system rules, norms, and practices was not the result of new power distributions but rather of new identities and social relations. New identities tend to develop during periods of rapid change when traditional institutions are challenged and legitimate authority undermined. In this case the victorious powers not only needed to adapt to a new distribution of capabilities but also to a new social structure in Europe. The new social changes in Europe were not the result of hegemonic war but rather of the French revolution.

The French revolution and its expansion undermined the political foundation of absolute monarchy and destroyed the political order that had governed the continent for several generations.[14] In addition to challenging monarchic rule, it also eroded the legitimacy of the Church and the aristocracy, the pillars underlying the ruling coalitions of Europe. Up to that point legitimacy had not been an important consideration in justifying state rule. Under the ancien régime hereditary succession had been a custom, generally an uncontested one. Only after dynastic continuity had been broken and the monarch's right to rule no longer taken for granted did it become an ideology.[15]

As Napoleon's armies swept across the continent, serfdom was abolished throughout central and eastern Europe and within the Italian peninsula. Ideas of citizenship and nationalism were institutionalized within the conquered territories through the Civil Code of Napoleon, threatening the foundations upon which most European monarchies were based. While the political elites and populations of Europe ultimately turned against Napoleon's empire, the ideals of the French revolution had taken root throughout the continent, not least within the Russian and Prussian ruling houses and among the political classes within the German principalities.[16]

The defeat of Napoleon ended the French bid for a continental empire, leaving to the victorious states the task of rebuilding the political and social structure of Europe. Twenty-five years of revolution, empire, and warfare left a very different continent from the one that had existed previously. Napoleon had abolished the Holy Roman Empire and either consolidated or reorganized most city-states and ancient republics into modern states. In all, the 234 territories that comprised the empire were reduced to 39 and placed under French rule.[17] When the Quadruple Alliance drove the French armies from the territories they had occupied, it left nearly half of Europe without government.[18] In many cases it was not clear who the legitimate rulers were or even which territories constituted states.[19]

All this presented a challenge to the European state system in a way that other major wars did not: even the victorious ruling regimes were concerned about their legitimacy in the new order.[20] This was reflected in a letter from French minister Talleyrand to the newly restored King Louis:

> What then is needed to give people confidence in legitimate authority? . . . Before the Revolution, power in France was restricted by ancient institutions, it was modified by the action of the large body of the magistracy, the clergy, and the nobility, who were necessary elements to its existence, and of whom it made use for the purpose of governing. Now that all these institutions are destroyed, and these great means of governing are annihilated, others must be found, of which public opinion will not disapprove.[21]

Tallyrand may have overstated the need to command public support at this point in history, however, he accurately reflected a belief among sovereigns that state authority in the new order needed to be based on some form of social consensus that was derived from commonly accepted principles of legitimacy. The coalition between crown and altar could not accomplish this any longer. Perhaps historian Guillaume de Bertier de Sauvigny's description of France's dilemma could serve as a general statement on the dilemma faced by all of the European states:

> The task of the new (post-Napoleonic) order in France was to fit the old monarchical, patriarchal, theocratic and feudal institution into the new Napoleonic, national, secular, and administrative state; to balance

the new society emerging from the Revolution with the old privileged classes who intended to reoccupy their places along with the king.[22]

Moreover, at a European level the revolution itself shook the diplomatic order like nothing else in the recent past. As Andreas Osiander argues, "If the thinking that had triumphed in the French Revolution has a basic message, it was that every custom, every social construct could be challenged. The international system, just as much as the domestic organization of the actors that made it up, was such a construct."[23]

As chaotic as the ancien régime seemed to be at times on the European level, two diplomatic institutions had provided a degree of stability and predictability in European relations: dynastic ties and the balance of power.[24] Both were severely challenged by the French revolution and Napoleon's empire.

Dynastic ties had created political and social bonds that cut across state boundaries, while the balance of power placed limits on the degree to which rulers could use these bonds to expand their domains. To the degree that monarchs created nonterritorial transnational connections with other monarchs through marriage and family compact, dynastic ties provided the framework for peacetime alliances. Rulers were conscious of their position as part of a transnational family and of their responsibilities to it.[25] Thus, throughout the era, the principle justification for territorial claims tended to be dynastic rights, symbolized by the common names for the wars: the Wars of Spanish Succession, Austrian Succession, Polish Succession, and Bavarian Succession.[26]

The balance of power provided a mechanism to restrain monarchs from using these practices to dominate the continent. This is why domestic succession disputes often escalated into European wars. Rulers recognized that the identity of a ruling house had international ramifications if that king had dynastic ties with the monarch in another state. Thus, all monarchs had an interest in the outcome of a domestic succession struggle. Monarchs who attempted to expand their domains through transnational compacts beyond a certain limit were met with opposition from other monarchs. This was the link between the dynastic and balance of power systems in the ancien régime.

The French revolution and Napoleon's empire undermined both systems. The effect of abolishing large numbers of states, absorbing others into the empire, and rending still others as satellites is obvious. More important, however, was the effect on the concept of legitimate statehood. The revolution introduced the concept of nationalism as a legitimizing principle for state rule, undermining not only the position of the monarchs but that of the European system as well. Raison d'état had linked the interests of the state with its monarch or dynastic family, not with any particular people or nationality. With the threat of nationalism, rulers needed to develop a new source of legitimacy, particularly in the large parts of Europe where Napoleonic administrations needed to be replaced.

Consequently, not only did the European monarchs need to develop a workable diplomatic and territorial system to regulate their relations with each other, the sovereigns themselves needed to relegitimize their rule domestically. If constitutionalism and nationalism were temporarily defeated with the victory over Napoleon, the ancien régime was so undermined that a simple "restoration" of the status quo ante was impossible. In sum, the French revolution inspired the ruling elites to seek new forms of legitimation and support to replace their domestic coalitions of crown and altar. One source was external: the monarchs could draw legitimacy from each other and from a European system that was based on what would soon be known as the "legitimist principle." These were the conditions that made the evolution of transnational identities possible.

Europeanism and the Concert of Vienna

Concert systems and common security associations both require a high level of commitment toward a greater good that goes beyond any notion of parochial self-interest. The common experiences of the previous twenty-five years—the French revolution, the Napoleonic wars, and the social and political reorganization of Europe—convinced the members of the Quadruple Alliance that it would be necessary to adopt a more systemic approach to reconstruction after the war was over. Osiander refers to this as a high degree of "system-consciousness," while Schroeder calls it "systemic thinking."[27] What made this kind of thinking conceivable, however, was a growing belief that Europe not only constituted a system but also a type of political community. By this I mean a recognition by the leadership of the Quadruple Alliance and the restored French monarchy of a social interdependence, a shared history, and a common culture that distinguished Europe as a unique society of states.

The development of a European consciousness grew largely out of the changes made by Napoleon in the social structure of Europe. Unlike previous and future European conflicts, the final war against France was not a conflict between alliances or dynastic families, rather it ultimately became a collective European struggle against a common enemy. With the formation of the fifth coalition Napoleon had no allies apart from those leaders he had installed within the conquered territories; by the end of 1813 all Europe north of the Alps was at war with Napoleon.[28] Thus the conflict became a continental crusade against a conqueror. This united Europe in a manner unseen since its wars against the Ottoman Empire several centuries before. Moreover, the sheer size of Napoleon's empire had physically united much of the continent into a single political unit. Between the French Empire, the Napleonic satellites, and Napoleon's pre-1813 allies, only Great Britain, Ireland, Portugal, and Sweden remained physically untouched by Napoleon's Europe.[29] By destroying the small petty states and consolidating them into large administrative units, Napoleon reduced the number of boundaries that divided the continent.

On another level the European state system provided a type of reference group that represented the values and ideals that domestic elites wished to promote and maintain within their own societies. The French revolution had made the European aristocracy increasingly conscious of their common bonds as a transnational ruling class. In the aftermath of the war the accessions of power and glory at the expense of another ruler were reduced in importance in proportion to their estimate of the threat involved in the French revolution.[30] Among the representatives at the Congress of Vienna this was particularly true of Austrian foreign minister Clements von Metternich, an aristocrat who saw Europe as representing tradition and stability in the face of radicalism and anarchy. To Metternich and others of the Austrian elite, liberalism was a transnational threat to the traditional European way of life. Moreover, Austria's multiethnic empire contained eleven nationalities; the revolutionary idea of nationalism threatened this system. As Metternich would later remark: "The only form of government which is suited to the concentration of peoples which makes up the Empire as a whole, is the monarchical form, because the cohesion of the parties would be absolutely impossible under a republican form of government."[31] As a result, Metternich believed that the only sure foundation of order lay in the monarchic principle and the principle of legitimacy, both of which became European concepts.[32] For Austria to remain independent and secure, Europe as a whole had to be independent and secure.[33]

This was equally true of the restored French monarchy. Although French foreign policy after the war was in part aimed at breaking away from the restraints imposed on it by the Quadruple Alliance, the government also realized that the Bourbon monarchy could only survive as part of a system of European monarchies.[34] To be a French monarch meant being a European one as well.

Russia also entered the postwar era needing to greater integrate itself into Europe. Its position as a great power was tied to its participation in European affairs. For a century Russia had sought recognition as a European power equal to the other great powers. Under Peter the Great Russia began to send young Russian noblemen abroad to study European politics and languages. This practice was continued by Catherine II and Paul I, who sought to overcome a lack of trained diplomatic bureaucracy by attaching young men to Russian embassies as a kind of diplomatic apprenticeship.[35] Consequently, by the end of the eighteenth century much of Russia's identity as a great power was conditioned upon its ties to the European state system. In this sense Russia learned how to operate as a nation-state in foreign affairs from its reference group, Europe. During this period Russian leaders began to see themselves and their country as part of a cosmopolitan aristocratic European community.

The sense of community with Europe—to which Russia was intricately bound both politically and culturally in the early nineteenth century—was internalized by the top foreign policy decision makers. As historian Patricia Kennedy Grimsted argues, "Through their common use of the French language, their similar social and cultural values, wealth and usually aristocratic blood or titles, Russia's diplomats belonged to the socioculturally, homogeneous European *corps diplomatique*."[36] It is for this reason that most of Alexander's foreign policy advisers were drawn from other states. For example Nesselrode was German, Kapodistrias Greek, Pozzo di Borgo Corsican, and Czartoryski Polish.[37] These advisers helped to make the Russian government more European.

Evidence for the development of a European identity can be found both through diplomatic discourse and the practices adopted by the Quadruple Alliance. With the formation of the fifth coalition the focus of the war expanded toward reestablishing a European order, or, in the words of article 16 of the Treaty of Chaumont, a "European equilibrium." This was evident in the way that the members of the alliance began speaking on behalf of Europe as a conceptual community. At the Council at Langres in February 1814, for example, the future allies claimed for the first time to be representing not only themselves but all of Europe.[38] This continued at the meeting in Chatillon, where the Quadruple Alliance was formally established. The allies issued a declaration that they had come not only as representatives of their respective states but also "as men entitled to treat for Peace with France in the name of Europe, which is but a single entity."[39]

Picking up on this theme, Prussian minister Schwarzenberg, in addressing a French gathering after the allies entered Paris in 1814, continually spoke in terms of Europe rather than of the alliance. "Europe wishes to be at peace with France," he told the crowd. "Europe does not wish to encroach on the rights of a great nation . . . and (Europe) wishes to disarm."[40] He just as easily could have spoke in the name of the alliance, since it was their armies that were then occupying France. He chose to evoke European legitimacy.

During this period Metternich had begun to develop a vision for a cosmopolitan (aristocratic) European society that equated the interests of each state with those of the continent.[41] Europe, Metternich said, "has acquired for me the quality of one's own country."[42] In his private papers Metternich revealed that he had seen himself as standing for the society of Europe since 1814.[43] Tsar Alexander was the most enthusiastic promoter of a Europeanist perspective. As the war ended he began to plan for a rationalized European society of states in which national governments were legitimized through constitutions granted by their sovereigns. Even French minister Talleyrand began to share this vision, describing Europe as "a society . . . a family . . . a republic of Princes and peoples."[44]

For the first time Britain had begun to see itself as politically tied to the management of peacetime continental affairs. Throughout Foreign Minister Castlereagh's negotiations with Austria and Russia, prior to the conference at Chaumont, he regarded himself as more than just a British minister promoting British interests; he saw himself as promoting the general interests of Europe.[45] Britain's policy would no longer be based on building alliances with particular states to prevent any single state from dominating but rather, for the first time, on participation in a general system of management in Europe.[46] For Castlereagh Europe had developed a "unity and persistence of purpose such as it had never before possessed."[47] Toward this end Castlereagh saw Britain's role at Vienna as that of arbiter for Europe.[48]

Whether this is evidence of a growing European identity is a matter of interpretation. The reconstruction of Europe, however, suggests that state practice was consistent with the discourse that had begun to dominate diplomatic relations. The strongest evidence is the Congress of Vienna itself. The Peace of Westphalia had established the practice of calling congresses to end major wars, therefore the idea of a conference was not unique. However, this was not to be a meeting of victorious states to discuss how to divide the spoils but rather a European-wide conference that would become the most comprehensive meeting of heads of states held to date.[49]

On one level the congress was a continental celebration by the aristocracy and monarchs marking what at the time appeared to be the defeat of the French revolution. Most of the event consisted of extravagant parties, formal dances, and opulent dinners. On another level it was an open meeting for the European political elites to discuss the reconstruction of the continent. Not only was the congress not restricted to the winning states, it included anyone who could claim to have an interest in the reconstruction of the continent. Besides the reigning monarchs and their ministers, a large number of diplomats representing old dynasties came to Vienna to claim their rights, bringing with them questions of succession. Even those sovereigns installed by Napoleon sent their delegates.

Such a gathering would be unnecessary, and in many ways counterproductive, if the goals were simply to reestablish a functional balance of power among the major powers and compensate the winning states. The victorious states could easily have imposed a settlement on Europe without the participation of other countries. Allowing other states to press their claims could only complicate the creation of a European balance and would certainly impinge on the ability of the victorious states to establish spheres of influence. Yet article 32 of the first Peace of Paris read, "All the Powers *engaged on either side in the present war* shall, within the space of two months, send Plenipotentiaries to Vienna for the purpose of regulating, in *General* Congress, the arrangements which are to complete the provisions of the present treaty."[50] Since virtually every country in Europe had been either occupied by, allied with, or opposed to Napoleon, the term "on either side of the present war" was an open invitation.

Several historians have commented on the way in which the great powers created a conceptual barrier around Europe during this period. Edward Gulick, for example, argues that the primary condition that gave rise to the Vienna settlement was a common European framework based on a shared historical legacy.[51] The pervasive heritage of cosmopolitanism led Europeans to think in continental, as opposed to strictly national, terms. Similarly, Paul Schroeder argues that the powers "fenced off" the European state system from the outside world, allowing them to ignore influences and issues that did not affect the continent itself.[52] This was reflected in the attempt by the great powers to develop a Europeanist approach toward reconstruction. That is, their interests and claims would be evaluated within the context of a general European settlement. Such an approach implies a group consciousness in the sense that "Europe" became the primary unit of analysis during the deliberations.

The adoption of this approach limited the alternatives that each state could pursue. In the first place it forced each of the ministers to reconcile their national claims with the interests of the continent. If a state wanted to promote its selfish interests, its representatives would have to demonstrate how that would help or at least not disrupt the new European order. The approach also created a dynamic whereby the ministers acted as partners rather than competitors in reconstruction. This did not prevent great power representatives from pursuing their own national claims, but it did limit the degree to which they could attempt to do so at the expense of the group. Moreover, it enabled them to overcome relative gains concerns in creating a general system of security and a balance of rights and responsibilities.

The Construction of a Great Power Club

The Congress of Vienna was originally called as a general meeting to resolve the outstanding territorial and diplomatic issues that were not settled in the Treaty of Paris. However, little thought had gone into how this would be accomplished. As delegates began to arrive in Vienna, they found that there was no procedure with which to conduct the congress. Moreover, it was unclear when the meeting would even begin, how decisions would be made, or who would be represented. The first secret article of the Treaty of Paris had stated that the dispensation of conquered territories would fall to the "allies."[53] Yet the war against Napoleon had been much broader than the members of the Quadruple Alliance, and *eight* countries had signed the Paris agreement. In fact, the Treaty of Chaumont itself was not exclusively an agreement among the original members of the alliance. Sweden, Spain, Portugal, and Holland all acceded to the treaty through a secret article, and thus they became signatories to the Quadruple Alliance. Consequently, it was not clear who would be defined as an allied power.

One way to resolve this question could have been through the formation of interest blocs by the principle states to increase bargaining leverage. If this avenue had been pursued, the criteria for whom to include in decision making would have been essentially ad hoc and opportunistic. The allies would seek to include those who they thought would either support their position or would cause problems for the others. During the negotiations leading to the Peace of Westphalia, for example, France and Sweden insisted that the princes of the Holy Roman Empire be included in negotiations, a move designed to weaken the bargaining position of the Hapsburgs.[54] This was a real possibility. German and Italian princes appealed to Tsar Alexander for help in realizing their national aspirations. With their support and Russia's overwhelming military resources on the continent, the tsar could have expanded Russia's power and become the unchallenged arbiter of Europe.[55] Moreover, the Swedish envoy, Gustavus von Löwenhjelm, was a protégé of Alexander, and was viewed as an ally.[56]

A second option could have been the formation of dynastic blocs among sovereigns with family ties. Many of the princes who had traditionally ruled the German and Italian states were related by marriage to sovereigns from the Quadruple Alliance. In fact, all of the major powers had dynastic ties to princes in other states in Europe. Territorial claims could have been made on the basis of compact. Balance of power dynamics would explain either outcome.

Neither of these options were pursued, however. Rather, the necessity of relegitimizing the state and building a workable diplomatic system for Europe encouraged the members of the Quadruple Alliance to attempt a consensus rather than engage in a competition for maximum advantage.[57] This, however, would not be easy. Despite their commitment to act not only as sovereign states but also as Europeans, the early meetings were characterized by tension and mistrust. Centuries of rivalry and hostility were part of the history of their relationships, and that could not help but affect the attitudes of the sovereigns and ministers toward each other. Moreover, Alexander and Metternich had a personal animosity that dated back to the conduct of the war against Napoleon.[58] In this sense the politics of realism played an important role in the congress. However, while structural theories can explain why historic rivals would be wary of each other after the hostilities had ceased, they do not account for the conditions under which these suspicions would ultimately be overcome. Thus, the story of the congress is not only about power politics and strategic interaction but also about the way the great powers came to view themselves as an exclusive club with the unique responsibility for managing the affairs of the continent.

The distinction between great and secondary powers emerged over time as the allies tried to determine who should be involved in the process of decision making, first at the Congress of Vienna and later at the Congress of Aix-la-Chapelle. In preparing the agenda for Vienna, the allies decided to create two decision-making bodies: a committee comprised of the self-defined "leading powers," first held to be the original members of the Quadruple Alliance plus France and Spain, and a broader eight-person committee comprised of the signatories of the Peace of Paris, which would also include Portugal and Sweden.[59] As the deliberations continued, however, it become apparent that the final directing cabinet for the conference would not be based on the Treaty of Paris as assumed, but on a conceptual distinction between "great" and "secondary" powers. Only those designated as a leading power would share membership in what was to become an exclusive club. This decision not only foreshadowed the decision-making process for the remainder of the congress, it would consolidate into a form of governance in which the great powers would collectively make decisions for the management of European affairs.

This was the first time in European diplomacy that a distinction had been had been made between leading and secondary powers.[60] It also marked the first time that the term *great power* would begin to be used as part of diplomatic phraseology.[61] Until that point it was generally accepted that all sovereign states were diplomatically equal, whatever their size or resources. Perceptions of strength certainly influenced the outcome of diplomacy, but no monarch was included or excluded on the basis of whether he was classified as a leading or great power. Rather decisions regarding who to include or exclude were usually made on the basis of realpolitik, that is, stacking the meeting with allies. As historian Charles Webster argues, the concept of leading powers "was an arbitrary distinction resting on no legal basis, asserting the claim of the Great Powers to have a special position in the European polity."[62]

There was no real criteria for applying the term *great power* to a particular nation, nor has one been devised since (although this distinction was made in practice when the United Nations Security Council was created). While political scientists and historians have often used the term, no one has been able to distinguish between a small great power and a large secondary one. As Jack Levy points out, "Scholars have either not attempted to define the concept or made no effort to translate vague definitions into operational criteria."[63] This is not an accident. The distinction between a great and secondary power is as much conceptual as it is structural. While there have always been strong and weak states, the Congress of Vienna was the first time this distinction had political as opposed to military or economic significance. Relying on objective structural criteria presents problems of definition. The Vienna great powers, for example, were, in Paul Schroeder's estimation, "a pentarchy composed of two superpowers [Britain and Russia], one authentic but vulnerable [and occupied] great power [France], one highly marginal and even more vulnerable great power [Austria] and one power called great by courtesy only [Prussia]."[64]

The only clear criterion for greatness, then, is the one that developed during the secret deliberations at Vienna: a power achieves this rank when acknowledged by others to have it.[65] In this case the members of the Quadruple Alliance, and later France, agreed among themselves that they constituted a special group of states with a distinctive set of rights and responsibilities for the governance of Europe. To the Austrian minister Metternich and the Russian tsar Alexander, great power supervision over the small powers—extending even to measures that could hardly be considered as external—seemed obvious and natural.[66] For British minister Castlereagh the need for a union of great powers was necessary, not only to guard against the danger from France (which was soon invited to join the union) but also for the general interests of Europe.[67] While power considerations can account for the ability of the Quadruple Alliance to assume the right to collectively rule Europe, it does not explain how they overcome their rivalries in order to do so.

The establishment of a *juste équilibre* necessitated a division of responsibility among the members of the group and in some cases involved strengthening some of the powers so that they could assume their role. Toward this end Castlereagh advocated "a substantial enlargement of Prussia," a suggestion accepted by all powers.[68] Under normal circumstances relative gains concerns should preclude this type of action. The argument that this was done simply to check Russian power is weak, since Prussia was Russia's staunchest ally at the congress. Rather, Prussia had a role in maintaining the vital "center" that was so fundamental to the new European order. Consistent with this, Alexander did not insist on being included in the "German Committee" that created the German confederation and a treaty of mutual defense. This is because the committee included only the major German states (such as Bavaria and Hanover), and was therefore led by Austria and Prussia.[69] Given Russia's traditional interest in central Europe—and its historic use of the German principalities to challenge Austrian power—Alexander's agreement to allow its two traditional rivals to have sole influence in this key strategic region offers at least circumstantial evidence that he accepted the idea of roles and responsibilities over strategic advantage within the club of great powers. If Russia was the hegemonic power on the continent, it certainly did not act like one.

It is for this reason that Russia encouraged a close partnership between Austria and Prussia, a radical departure from its "divide and conquer" strategy of the eighteenth century. Thus, the interests of the small powers could be sacrificed to achieve an equilibrium, and no attempt was made by any of the great powers to bring them in as allies against each other. This conscious and deliberate creation of a European equilibrium by enlarging some states and giving out spheres of responsibility to others is inconsistent with Grieco's neorealist "positional theory."[70] I would suggest that their decision to act like Europeans and great powers helped them to overcome the relative gains problem that would theoretically preclude such an approach. Certainly there were strong differences among the great powers as to what constituted an equilibrium, however the commitment toward a collective solution constrained the possible alternatives that the powers could pursue.

As argued in chapter 2, social groups exhibit a degree of closure that ties one's definition of self in part to that of the broader group. By conceptually dividing Europe into great (the self) and secondary (the other) powers, the great powers established a new role for themselves, based on a collective understanding that they shared a special and unique status. In this sense their prestige was tied to their membership in a collective body. This understanding would be strengthened by a variety of titles that would come to identify them as a distinct group: "Union of Principle Powers," "Union of Great Powers," "Leading Powers," "Aristocracy of Great Powers," "Union of Chief Sovereigns," "Powers of the First Rank," and "Powers of the First Order." As such, the powers had begun to identify their interests with those of the group. As Prussian foreign minister Friedrich Ancillon would later comment:

> The five great powers, closely united among themselves and with the others, form a system of solidarity by which one stands for all and all for one; in which power appears only as protection for everybody's possessions and rights; in which the maintenance of the whole and the parts within legal bounds, for the sake of the peace of the world, has become the only aim of political activity.[71]

Similarly, Austrian publicist Friedrich Von Gentz, the secretary of the congress, described "the five great powers as the protector of the federation of European states."[72] This view was echoed by Castlereagh, who stated that "the Great Powers feel that they have not only a common interest, but a common duty to attend to."[73] Exaggerated and idealistic words to be sure, but they also reflected the sentiment that had begun to develop among a select group of states.

If sovereignty, geopolitics, and historic rivalry brought the great powers into potential conflict during the congress, what brought them together as a unique social group? In the first place, they shared a common characteristic that differentiated them from other states: the political, military, economic, and geographic resources to manage the affairs of the continent. This characteristic, however, only gained meaning within the context of the group. None of the powers could individually accomplish this task, nor could they form combinations that would provide the resources necessary to oversee continental security. Systems management was a collective task in which each piece was necessary for the functioning of the whole.

As a result, each power was given a sphere of responsibility. Austria and Prussia's identity as German states would enable them to jointly manage the German confederation, Austria's dynastic ties to several of the Italian princes helped it to manage the north Italian states, Russia's size and historic ties to eastern Europe made them the obvious power to oversee eastern and southeastern Europe, and Britain's historic role as protector the low countries and the Iberian peninsula made it the pillar in the west.

Second, the great powers recognized a positive interdependence among themselves. For the British there was a new recognition that they were politically tied to the management of peacetime continental affairs, a radical departure from Britain's historic insular relationship with Europe. As Castlereagh noted in a letter:

> In the present state of Europe it is the province of Great Britain to turn the confidence she has inspired to the account of peace, by exercising a conciliatory influence between the Powers, rather than put herself at the head of any combinations of Courts to keep others in check. . . . The immediate object to be kept in view is to inspire the States of Europe, as long as we can, with a sense of the dangers which they have surmounted by their union . . . and that their true wisdom is to keep down the petty contentions of ordinary times, and to stand together in support of the established principles of social order.[74]

For Austria, Prussia, France, and Russia there was a positive interdependence based on a form of monarchic solidarity. Recognizing the impact of the French revolution on the legitimacy of monarchy and the aristocracy, the great power monarchs realized that their fortunes were linked. For Tallyrand, a European equilibrium required that the legitimacy of *all* thrones be acknowledged and recognized.[75] A European order based on this "legitimist principle" would strengthen the institutions of monarchy domestically against the transnational movements of nationalism and liberalism. By making a conceptual distinction between traditional monarchic states (the self) and radical liberal ones (the other), the monarchies developed a transnational bond that united them.

Metternich, long regarded as one of the great masters of realpolitik, believed that the ultimate survival of the Austrian monarchy rested in a close association with other monarchies. Metternich preferred the maintenance of strong monarchies to the maintenance of treaties as a way to guarantee stability.[76] "Political repose rests on fraternization between monarchs," Metternich argued, "and on the principle of maintaining that which is. To oppose these fundamental principles would be to shake the edifice to its very foundation."[77] For this reason Metternich and Prussian minister Hardenberg both agreed that the agenda of the congress would include the regulation of relations between rulers and subjects and other social questions running across Europe.[78]

These shared characteristics were highlighted by their common experience in dealing with the aftermath of the French Revolution and the subsequent war against Napoleon. Even before the rise of Napoleon, the major powers recognized the threat of the revolution to the established order and deployed troops to restore the deposed monarch. In 1793 the armies of the German princes invaded France from the north and east, and British forces attacked from the south and west.[79] While the Prussian and Russian ruling houses initially sympathized with the revolution, they too eventually turned against the Jacobins and joined the great power crusade.

The final war against Napoleon had brought the great power leaders together in an unusually close collaboration. The allied sovereigns lived a common life for almost two years, and there existed between them something of the spirit of connection and obligation that binds individuals and nations together when faced with a common task or threat.[80] During this period they became accustomed to close cooperation; they traveled together for hundreds of miles, saw each other daily, and grew accustomed to dealing with foreign affairs much in the same way as they were used to tackling domestic affairs.[81] As Metternich noted in his *Memoirs*:

> By a coincidence which was not only singular at the time but without example in the annals of history, the chief personages in the great drama found themselves together in the very same place. The Emperors of Austria and Russia, the King of Prussia, and their three cabinets, were really never separated. The leader of the English cabinets had also generally been with his colleagues of Austria, Russia and Prussia.[82]

Moreover, in assuming the leadership of the final coalition and subsequently the responsibility for facilitating the reconstruction of Europe, they acted as "trustees" for the continent. This created a unique relationship between the powers that was not shared by any other state.

None of this is to imply that the congress was free of conflict. During discussions over the most controversial issue, the dispensation of Poland and Saxony, the great powers threatened to form rival blocs. For a short time mutual animosity was great and tension was high. Yet neither question broke up the congress or divided Europe. Nor did they have any lasting effects on the relations among the great powers, who continued to work at a collective approach toward reconstruction. A compromise was reached within a month of the crisis, and the issue was never revisited again. This suggests that even under the most adverse conditions the great powers were able to maintain their essential unity.

The Concert of Europe and the Congress System

If the Concert of Europe was a security regime formed on the basis of mutual self-interest, its development should have been the result of multilateral negotiation and strategies of reciprocity. Moreover, one should be able to demonstrate that the institution was *designed* to fulfill anticipated functions.[83] In the alternative, if it was the outcome of power politics, we should be able to trace the process through which hegemonic powers imposed it on the others or at least explain how it was designed to counter anticipated threats. Neither of these conditions, however, were present.

The concert was not formed either through a negotiated agreement or a treaty of alliance. Nor was it imposed on Austria, Prussia, and France by the dominant powers of Europe, Britain, and Russia. Rather, it emerged over time from a general practice of consultation and a recognition by the great powers that they shared a common relationship that defined them as a social group. Specifically, it was through their practice of dealing with European-wide issues collectively from 1814 through 1823 (and beyond) that the *general* nature of their relationship became increasingly clear. As Richard Elrod argues, concert diplomacy actively cultivated the conception of the great powers as a unique and special peer group.[84] In this sense the congresses (the practice) created the concert (the institution), rather than the other way around, a phenomenon not accounted for in liberal institutionalist theory.

While the possibility of holding periodic meetings was provided for in both the treaty of the Quadruple Alliance and the Second Peace of Paris, their conception was vague, and there were no plans to call any.[85] Article 5 of the Second Peace of Paris (which called for a future meeting of the allies) was inserted to provide a method for ending the occupation of France. In fact, the original idea of holding meetings was primarily a convenient diplomatic expedient for facilitating the common action of the allies on specific questions; they were not considered as part of an ongoing system.[86] Moreover, with the restoration of King Louis to the throne of France, the revolutionary threat from France diminished. There was no apparent security threat or convergence of interest that can account for the evolution of the concert.

The Concert of Europe was an unintended outcome of the political dynamics that emerged during the period surrounding the Congress of Aix-la-Chapelle, whose purpose was to end the occupation of France. By 1818 France had paid off its indemnity and established domestic stability under a set of monarchic institutions. With the expiration of the three-year occupation provided for in the Treaty of Paris, Russia proposed a congress to discuss terminating the occupation of France and other general issues relating to the European community. The other powers were eager to end the occupation and agreed with the need for a meeting to finalize the terms.[87] Although there was some discussion about allowing the secondary states to participate, ultimately all the great powers agreed to maintain the closed club that they had established at Vienna. Informally, they decided to act as trustees for European security by initiating a series of ongoing meetings and congresses to deal with all issues of European importance. This, I would argue, displays a collective consciousness of themselves as an exclusive and cohesive group.

The decision to maintain great power unity would later be reinforced at the conference through a series of public and private declarations that Europe would be governed by the five great powers. The protocol adopted by the powers on November 15, 1818, sounded more like a group compact than a collective defense agreement or treaty of alliance. The fact that this protocol was a *secret*, rather than a public, statement issued by the great powers suggests that it was not dispatched for public relations purposes. For example:

> The five Powers . . . are firmly resolved never to depart, neither in their mutual Relations, nor in those which bind them to other states, from principles of intimate union which hitherto presided over all their common relations and interests, a union become more strong

and indissoluble from the bonds of Christian brotherhood which join them.[88]

As great powers, they would continue to speak in terms of their collective trusteeship over the continent. In a joint declaration publicly issued to the European community they stated that:

> The intimate Union established among the Monarchs, who are joint parties to the System, by their own principles, no less than by the interests of their peoples, offer to Europe the most sacred pledge of its future tranquillity.[89]

The fact that they spoke in lofty idealistic terms is not in and of itself significant; few nations justify their actions in terms of their own interests alone. What is interesting is the fact that they saw an "intimate union" of the great powers as the vehicle for achieving these seemingly idealistic goals. This union was not to be a traditional balancing alliance; all the major powers were grouped together. As Austrian adviser Friedrich Gentz described it:

> [The Great Power princes are] the protectors and preservers of public order; their intimate union . . . is the counterpoise to the disorder which turbulent spirits try to bring into human affairs; the nucleus of organized strength which this union presents is the barrier which Providence itself appears to have raised to preserve the old order of society.[90]

This was at least a rhetorical departure from the doctrine of realpolitik, which holds that ultimately only self-reliance can guarantee one's security and independence. Instead, these statements identify their interests as sovereign states with those of great powers *as a group*, an indication of a group consciousness that can not be explained by realpolitik. Bringing an outside state into the inner circle of the group would diminish the distinction between great and secondary powers. It was this exclusivity that made group cohesion possible, and it became an accepted norm never to break the "magic circle of the elite and powerful."[91] Over the next few decades three more congresses and many more great power consultations were held to discuss issues relating to European politics. In each case, the great powers maintained their solidarity against involving the secondary states, even in the face of strong disagreements among themselves.

In the post-Napoleonic order being a great power meant accepting certain norms of behavior and principles of conduct in one's relations with other great powers. Where did these norms come from? The answer to this question suggests which interpretation of the concert is most accurate. Norms can emerge from a variety of sources. First, they can be imposed on the system by hegemonic powers. I would call these realist norms in the sense that they are derivative of power relations.[92] Second, they can be negotiated by coequal partners seeking to develop a workable system of cooperation and collaboration.[93] These are regulative norms and are most consistent with institutionalist theories, particularly regimes. Finally, they can develop organically within a community or social group as a reflection of the identity of the group itself. These are social or constitutive norms.[94]

The norms that defined acceptable behavior within the concert were of the third type. There is no evidence that these standards of behavior were imposed on the group by either Britain or Russia, the two dominant powers. It is not even clear why such norms would reflect their interests apart from a belief in group solidarity. Nor is there any indication that the five powers explicitly negotiated them for some functional purpose. Moreover, they were not codified as legal rules but rather developed over time through ongoing practice, in particular through the interactions of the great powers at Vienna and Aix-la-Chapelle. The norms and principles that were the foundation of the concert system reflected the identity of the group. As argued in chapter 2, social identities carry with them a certain range of prerogatives and obligations that an actor who is accorded that identity may carry out. The common transnational identity of great powers facilitated certain expectations of behavior from which more explicit rules eventually developed.

The first principle held that the management of European affairs was a collective responsibility and therefore no power could attempt to settle a European question by an independent initiative.[95] This was the principle of group cohesion. This held even in cases where a state's traditional interests were at stake, such as Austria in Italy and Russia's relationship with the Ottoman Empire. The members of the concert accepted constraints on their right to self-help because their role as a great power required them to do so. To do otherwise would have threatened the very system they sought to maintain. As trustees over European affairs, they defined their interests partly in terms of the common good.

Great power cohesion was maintained in part through the newly developed concept of grouping. Grouping was a mechanism to restrain destabilizing adventures and aggressive behavior, not by balancing potential threats with a blocking alliance but by committing all powers to adhere to group norms and restraints. As Jervis argues, the great powers decided that potentially menacing states could best be contained by keeping them close to the group.[96] Thus whenever an issue of European interest arose it became natural to call a meeting or congress to discuss a collective response. Sometimes the response would involve action by only one of the powers, as in the cases of the Spanish and Italian revolutions, but in virtually every instance the support and sanction of the group was required.

While each of the powers at one time tried to avoid the constraints of the group by attempting unilateral action, the norms of the great power concert eventually forced them to seek collective approval before any action was taken. In fact, the only way a power could avoid group involvement was to convince the other great powers that the issue was local rather than European in nature. Thus, the way in which the powers defined each situation largely determined their expected behavior and their range of options. For example, when Austria and Prussia responded to unrest in the German states by issuing the Carlsbad Decrees in 1819, the other powers saw them as acting within their roles as co-leaders of the German confederation and therefore did not get involved.[97] Thus their situated identities proscribed a specific range of expected behaviors.

This is related to a second primary norm: that great powers must not be humiliated and that they must not be challenged either in their vital interests or in their prestige and honor.[98] While this was in part a functional mechanism for preventing the rise of dissatisfied powers, it was also fundamental to group cohesion. No such concern was evident for nonmember states whose potential dissatisfaction could lead to war. For example, during the Eastern crises in the 1820s, the great powers were not concerned to avoid a humiliation of the Ottoman Empire. Their only concern was to avoid its destruction.[99] Similarly, when the great powers intervened to support Belgian independence from the Netherlands, they did not offer compensation to the Dutch the way they did to Prussia and Austria at the Congress of Vienna.

Third, great powers were expected not to pursue territorial ambitions, not to take advantage of the short-run vulnerabilities of each other, not to form rival blocs or combinations in opposition to other great powers, and not to consort with secondary powers to support their positions. In short, as trustees of continental stability and order, they could not act to disrupt it for national gain. In this sense the great powers collectively acted as a reference group from which individual state leaders could evaluate each other's actions. Metternich's declaration of the need to maintain "the most absolute solidarity [among the great powers] in all questions of general interest"[100] was a reflection of this group consciousness.

The greatest test of group cohesion came in 1821 in an area of vital interest to Russia: the principalities within the Ottoman Empire. In March of that year Aleksandr Ipsilantis led a nationalist revolt against the Ottoman government in the Danube Principalities, hoping to spark a war that would destroy the Ottoman Empire and gain Greek independence. At first all five great powers opposed the rebellion as another threat to established authority.[101] This view changed after the Turkish authorities publicly executed the Christian patriarch of Constantinople on Easter Sunday. Russia had assumed the role of protector of the Eastern Orthodox Christians within the Ottoman Empire ever since the Treaty of Kutchuk-Kainardji in 1774. The Ottoman Empire was an Islamic theocracy, and thus the execution of a major Christian religious leader turned the conflict into a holy war. Within two months Russia had broken off diplomatic relations with the Ottomans.

At that point the great powers were convinced that war would soon follow, a course of action that all except Russia wished to avoid. Alexander wanted to help the Greeks but only on the basis of a European mandate, much as the one given to Austria in Naples (which I discuss later in this chapter).[102] Thus, when Alexander accepted Metternich's suggestion for a meeting of great power ministers at Vienna to discuss the affair, he was abandoning a principle of Russian diplomacy observed since the time of Catherine II — the principle of not permitting the interference of foreign powers in the relations between Russia and Turkey.[103] In fact, Russia did not go to war against Turkey in 1822, despite widespread provocation. Instead it agreed to treat the Greek issue within a general European settlement.[104] The willingness of Russia to acquiesce to the collective against its traditional interests is perhaps the strongest evidence of group loyalty. As Paul Schroeder argues, Alexander acted mainly to save the European alliance and for this he was willing to forego the likely gains of a legally justified war and accept the risk that Russia's influence would decline in the Near East relative to Austria and Britain.[105]

As an institution of great power collaboration, the Concert of Europe continued in at least a weak form until the Crimean War in 1854. While the practice of holding formal congresses among all five great powers declined after 1823, the key ingredients that helped to define the concert remained: the great powers did not pursue unilateral action, they consulted each other on all issues of European importance even where their vital issues were involved, and they did not form military alliances or rival blocs even after the Russian-Turkish war of 1828. What changed was not great power rule per se, but rather the *form* of rule. The rise of the Holy Alliance as a common security association promoting monarchic solidarity became the dominant institution in European politics.

Monarchic Solidarity and the Holy Alliance

While the Concert of Europe had provided for a form of governance based upon Great Power rule of Europe and political equilibrium among states, the Holy Alliance was designed to maintain a particular social structure within Europe based on monarchic solidarity. It clearly fits the definition of a common security association discussed in chapter 1. The treaty of the Holy Alliance, concluded in Paris on September 26, 1815, stated in part that

> the three contracting Monarchs [Austria, Russia and Prussia] will remain united by the bonds of a true and indissoluble fraternity, and considering each other as fellow countrymen, they will on all occasions and in all places lend each other aid and assistance. [They] consider themselves all as members of one and the same Christian nation; the three allied Princes looking on themselves as merely delegated by Providence to govern three branches of the One family, namely, Austria, Prussia, and Russia.[106]

Unlike a treaty of alliance, the Holy Alliance was to be a general association promoting the unity of Christian monarchs and the sanctity of royal institutions. The goals as written were as broad as they were vague. While Castlereagh derided the document as "a piece of sublime mysticism and nonsense," and Metternich initially referred to it as a "high sounding nothing,"[107] it would later become the symbolic representation of an evolving transnational identity among absolutist monarchs. Its goal would be to provide mutual assistance to monarchs challenged by nationalist and liberal rebellions.

The Holy Alliance was originally one of the most advanced ideas of its time.[108] The many references to religion, Christian brotherhood, and "exalted truths" should not obscure the political impact of the document. In Alexander's mind the alliance would bind the monarchs together in a general association for the purpose of guaranteeing the principles of public law, that is, the state of possession and the legitimacy of thrones.[109] Reflecting this bond, the document states:

> Considering each other as fellow countrymen, they will on all occasions and in all places lend each other aid and assistance. In consequence, the sole principle in force whether as between the said Governments or as between their subjects, shall be that of doing each other reciprocal service.[110]

Its purpose, then, was not to promote *state* power but rather *monarchic* power, a transnational value that tied specific domestic institutions to those of other states.

The evolution of the Holy Alliance into a union for the preservation of absolute monarchy *against* liberal change is all the more interesting considering that until 1819 Alexander insisted that granting liberal constitutions was the logical outcome of the sacred principles to which the signatories had subscribed.[111] Prior to the final signing, however, Metternich succeeded in altering the original text by eliminating some of the religious references and changing the thrust of the document into an attack on the transformations brought about by the French revolution.[112] Interestingly, only the three Eastern monarchs were sponsors of the treaty, although all monarchs except the sultan of the Ottoman Empire were invited to adhere to it. This was the first indication that the three powers who were bitter enemies for at least a century would find among themselves a special bond not shared by the other states.

It was not only the rule of law and the demands of necessity that guided the Holy Alliance; it was a belief in a duty to aid any legal and legitimate — that is monarchic — authority that was challenged by liberal and/or revolutionary forces. As Metternich stated in a letter to Prussian minister Wittgenstein: "Political repose rests on fraternization between monarchs [rather than military alliance] and on the principle of maintaining that which is. To oppose these fundamental principles would be to shake the edifice to its very foundation."[113] The idea of a common monarchic identity by the three Eastern powers as the basis for a coalition was articulated by Metternich in a letter to Alexander:

> Respect for all that is; liberty for every government to watch over the well-being of its own people; a league of all governments against factions in all states; refusal on the part of every monarch to aid or succor

partisans under any mask whatever—such are the ideas of the great monarchies. . . . Union between the monarchs is the basis of the policy which must now be followed to save society from total ruin.[114]

. . .

The first principle to be followed by the monarchs, united as they are by the coincidence of their desires and opinions, should be that of maintaining the stability of political institutions . . . let the great monarchs strengthen their union and prove to the world that if it exists, it is beneficent, and ensures the political peace of Europe.[115]

In another letter he continued his thoughts on the solidarity of monarchs:

Never has the world shown examples of union and solidarity in great political bodies like those given by Russia, Austria, and Prussia in the course of the last few years. By separating carefully the concerns of self-preservation from ordinary politics and by subordinating all individual interests to the common and general interest, the monarchs have found the true means of maintaining their holy union and accomplishing the enormous good which they have accomplished.[116]

While discourses are often manipulated for strategic reasons, they also reflect a trend in the way political leaders conceptualize themselves and their neighbors.[117] In this case we see a clear pattern among the ministers and sovereigns of the Eastern powers that indicates some consciousness of commonality around monarchic solidarity. Their national interests were at least partly tied to the institutions of monarchy, which were European in nature. In this sense the Holy Alliance was a reference group through which the ruling monarchs could justify their form of state to potential domestic challengers. This corresponds to the tone of political discourse that had begun to characterize this period. The three Eastern monarchies spoke of the peace of Europe in terms of preventing social revolution rather than guarding against the ambitions and aggressions of other states.

In reality, the Holy Alliance, as it came to be known in European politics, did not emerge from either a treaty or an idea but rather from political practice. Like the Concert of Europe, the Holy Alliance evolved over time. The transformation of the alliance from a "high sounding nothing" into an institution representing monarchic solidarity was the result of an ongoing interaction among the original signers. Once again, the practice preceded the institution. In fact, Russia continued to view the Holy Alliance as a vehicle to promote constitutionalism throughout Europe until at least 1819.[118] It was not until the Holy Alliance began to manifest itself in actual practice—in Spain, Piedmont, and Naples—that Alexander would eventually move away from his advocacy of constitutionalism toward support for Eastern absolutism.

The first opportunity for action by the Holy Alliance was in response to the Spanish revolution. In January 1820 Spanish troops destined for duty in the rebellious South American colonies revolted against King Ferdinand VII. Within two months the rebels had established a new government, compelling the king to restore the ultraliberal constitution of 1812. While Alexander still held sympathy for constitutionalism, his support for such charters was based on the idea that they would emanate from royal will not revolution. Thus, in April, the tsar proposed that the great powers jointly intervene in Spain to return the legitimate king to his throne and called for a congress to discuss this action.

The Spanish revolution embodied Metternich's worst fears of liberalism and anarchy. At the same time, he believed that the location of Spain at the farthest western reaches of the continent and the probability that the revolution would burn itself out mandated caution.[119] Castlereagh similarly opposed joint action on the grounds that the Spanish revolution was not a threat to the peace of Europe and was thus a local, not a European, issue. There was not a consensus to call a congress.

However, a military revolt in Naples four months later caused Austria to reevaluate its initial classification of the Spanish revolution as a local issue. Although the Congress of Vienna had designated Italy as part of Austria's sphere of responsibility, Metternich wanted to crush the rebellion with the support (but not the participation) of the other European great powers. Russia and France agreed to support Austria, but argued that this, like Spain, was a revolutionary challenge to the European order and therefore required a joint response, even if the troops used were to be Austrian.[120] Austria tried to deal with the issue by more informal means, however the norms of the great power concert clearly placed this issue on the European agenda.[121] Thus, although Austria did not want the other powers to place constraints on its ability to act, consultation was mandatory and the Congresses of Troppau and Laibach were born. Now Austria would be grouped.

Britain supported Austrian intervention but wanted it to act unilaterally on the basis of its treaties rather than as the head of an antirevolutionary European force.[122] The British thereby indicated that they would only send an observer to the congress. This presented a dilemma for Austria. Metternich and Emperor Francis knew that holding the congress would alienate England as a potential ally. Yet Austria chose to maintain its ties with the union of Eastern monarchs over the potential benefits of a British-Austrian alliance because, as Metternich stated, "of all the evils, the greatest would be to see Emperor Alexander abandon the moral tie which unites us and thus to set himself up again as the power protecting the spirit of innovation," that is, liberalism.[123] In this sense Austria valued the monarchic union over a potential strategic relationship with England, and this would help to reinforce the cohesion of the group.

At the Congress of Troppau the monarchs determined that the nature of a state's domestic institutions would be a key criteria for maintaining membership in the European system. They justified intervention on the grounds that domestic revolution was by definition a breach of the peace.[124] It is interesting to note that the Holy Alliance held revolution itself to be a breach, not just revolutions that threatened to expand. The rebellions that had recently occurred were not within countries that could pose a military threat. Spain, Portugal, Naples, and Piedmont were hardly states that could launch a Napoleonic-type war against Europe. However, Gentz argued that the European federation of states was like a body and revolution a disease that, once it had established itself in any part, might spread to the rest of the organism. As Metternich said, "The principle sovereigns were protector and keepers of the existing public order."[125] In the view of the Eastern powers, the social conflict in Europe transcended the political issues between states.[126]

Britain was at least as concerned as the Eastern powers with European stability and with maintaining the territorial arrangements forged at Vienna. However, it did not view liberal revolution as inherently destabilizing, a reflection of the strong support for liberalism that existed within the British Parliament. In his famous state paper issued prior to the congress, Castlereagh argued that the Quadruple Alliance had opposed France during the war not because of the democratic principles of the French Revolution but because of the military character it had assumed. The great powers, he urged, should confine its activities to protecting the peace and security of Europe, not protecting domestic monarchies.[127] This was the issue that divided Britain from the Holy Alliance.

While Metternich had hoped to maintain the unity of the great powers, it became clear at Troppau that he and Emperor Francis would have to choose between the support of Britain and that of Russia. They opted for a "special partnership" between the three Eastern monarchs.[128] Thus the Holy

Alliance would now take on a practical political expression as a bond of absolutist monarchs. The identity of "European great power monarch" had an existence independent of the states that shared it. Metternich instinctively understood this when he later stated that "the Alliance in its true acceptation is indestructible, it is political morality. . . . The alliance cannot perish; *it would exist without allies.*"[129] The function of the alliance was to preserve the social structure of Europe by maintaining domestic political regimes.[130] This would require the three powers to expand their definitions of national interest to include a commitment toward maintaining European monarchy.

The nature of discourse that began to dominate the internal discussions and public pronouncements of the Holy Alliance suggests that its members did indeed share a common identity as great power monarchs. Their shared identity was facilitated by a conceptual cleavage between monarchy and liberalism, tradition and revolution. Thus, Gentz spoke of the "solidarity of monarchs against the universal character of revolutionary movements," thereby superseding the vertical divisions between the members of the state system.[131] Similarly, in a letter to French prime minister Richelieu, Russian minister Capo d'Istria defined the cleavage as follows: "On the one side we see a consoling prospect of a real fraternity between the states and the gradual perfections of social institutions; on the other there appears the formidable empire of anarchy and revolutionary despotism."[132] This served as the basis for intervention by the Holy Alliance in suppressing several revolutions.

As a result, the political center of Europe shifted toward the Troppau alliance and its objective to support all "legitimate" governments against revolutionary movements.[133] The circumstances surrounding the interventions by the Holy Alliance are quite revealing in demonstrating how participation in the alliance changed the states' willingness to act as a group. The agreement by the alliance to sponsor an Austrian interventionary army into Naples to suppress the revolution and restore the original government showed a deference to Austria's sphere of responsibility. However, the sponsorship of its intervention in Piedmont soon after was more interesting, since Piedmont was not part of Austria's sphere. In another time it would have been extremely unlikely that the other powers, particularly Russia, would support an extension of Austrian military power outside of its domain.

At the same time, although Austria prized its hegemony in Italy, Metternich and Emperor Francis asked Tsar Alexander to supplement Austrian forces by providing ninety thousand Russian soldiers to crush an insurrection in Alesandria and Turin. This would have involved Russian troops crossing through Austria, a bold move requiring trust from a state that was still wary of Russian power.[134]

As it turned out, Austria did not need Russian help; they defeated the rebels within a matter of weeks. Yet the idea of Austria asking Russia to march its troops through central Europe into its sphere of responsibility was unprecedented in peacetime. Moreover, whatever Metternich's private ambitions may have been, Austria did not use its intervention to try to annex territory or bring Piedmont into Austria's sphere.[135] Following the restoration of the king, Austrian troops left.

Meanwhile the situation in Spain became more precarious for King Ferdinand, who asked the Holy Alliance to restore the power of the monarchy. Although Austria initially tried to discourage united allied action in Spain, it soon abandoned that position.[136] The post-Restoration liberal period in France had abruptly come to an end in December 1821 when the moderate Richelieu regime fell, bringing in a new ultraroyalist government. Thus, when King Ferdinand asked France for assistance in regaining power, the Ultras pressured the ministry to aid the royalist forces.[137] While the French elites welcomed the opportunity to reassert themselves in Europe, the government was badly split between the ultraroyalists—such as Foreign Minister Viscount Montmorency, who wanted to intervene—and the moderate royalists—like Prime Minster Jean Villèle, who believed that intervention would compromise French interests.[138]

They were also split on the degree to which the Spanish revolution should become a European issue. Villèle did not want France's decisions to be constrained by the Holy Alliance, however, Montmorency wanted the moral support of Europe before engaging in action in Spain.[139] For the Ultras the Holy Alliance was a reference group from which they could draw legitimacy. A European intervention on behalf of monarchy would help to justify and strengthen their monarchic position. Ultimately, however, it did not matter. Like Austria in Italy, this *was* a European issue and France would thus have to obtain the support of the other great powers to take action. The cost of France's membership in the European great power pentarchy was adherence to group norms. Once again the norms would prevail, and it was France's turn to be grouped. The result was the Congress of Verona.

The new French government sent Montmorency to the conference with instructions to keep the issue from being framed as a European question. It was not to be. Tsar Alexander had proposed the creation of a European army to invade Spain on behalf of the Holy Alliance. While there was little support for this proposal, Russian representative Dmitri Talischev, Metternich, and Prussian representative Gunther von Bernstorff agreed among themselves that "France must consider herself an agent of the Grand Alliance and that the question of Spain was entirely European."[140] Representing the Ultras more than the prime minister, Montmorency agreed and stated that France was "above all convinced that the concurrence of the great powers is necessary in order to preserve that unanimity of views which is the fundamental character of the alliance, and which it is of the utmost importance to maintain and emphasize as a guarantee for the repose of Europe."[141] While Villèle viewed this as a violation of his instructions, Montmorency enjoyed the support of the French delegation at Verona as well as most of the cabinet.[142]

Although the meetings were contentious, Metternich was determined to preserve the intimate alliance of the Eastern monarchies at any cost.[143] Citing the legitimist principle, the four powers formally attending the Congress of Verona (Britain sent representatives as observers) pledged action in the case of "a formal act of the Spanish (rebel) government infringing the rights of the legitimate succession of the Royal family."[144] With a European mandate to restore the royal government, France was now free to invade Spain without opposition from the other powers.[145] For the second time in a decade France invaded Spain, but this time the intervention was considered legitimate and approved by the monarchic alliance (although France claimed to be acting on its own). By August the French prevailed, and the liberal experiment in Spain came to an end.

Why did the European powers allow Bourbon France to invade Spain in order to restore another Bourbon to power? Theoretically, such an act should have sparked a balancing coalition against France. In fact, the European War of the Spanish Succession in the eighteenth century was fought over this very issue. In the same vein, why did the great powers support a French invasion of its neighbor less than five years after it was released from great power tutelage? Technically the treaty of the Quadruple Alliance was still in force, committing the other four powers to respond to such an action through military force.

What made this action possible was the sanction by the union of absolute monarchs. This was a war for the preservation of monarchy, not one of expansion. Once again, it was the definition of the situation, rather than an abstract concern with relative power, that identified the action as nonthreatening to the other powers. Although France conducted the war on its own, it was acting within its prescribed role as a great power monarch. Relative gains concerns were not a factor, and thus the other states did not react to an assertion of French power.

The preceding case illustrates how the development of common social identities can help states to overcome long-standing rivalries and establish cohesive security arrangements. None of the prevailing theories in security studies—balance of power, hegemony, alliance, deterrence, or regime—can adequately explain why a concert system and a common security association emerged in nineteenth-century Europe. The Napoleonic wars changed the distribution of capabilities in Europe in favor of Britain and Russia at the expense of France, but there is no evidence that either security arrangement was derivative of the hegemons' interests. While hegemony theories could explain why the Eastern states would sign Alexander's Holy Alliance document, they can not explain why the alliance ultimately reflected the interests of Austria more than Russia.

Neither were these institutions consciously *designed* by the great powers to solve specified coordination problems, the key condition that would support a liberal institutionalist explanation. Rather, they *evolved* over time from specific forms of interaction by states that began to view themselves as an exclusive group. Both the patterns of discourse and the observed behavior of the great powers were consistent with a social group sharing a common identity. While the politics of realism continued to play a role in their relationships, the five states continually approached the major issues as Europeans, great powers, and monarchs rather than only as Britains, Russians, Prussians, Austrians, and French.

If the system was structurally bipolar, as some historians argue it was, neither Russia nor Britain acted like bloc leaders.[146] They did not compete for supremacy in Europe, nor did they attempt to balance each other's power. Most important, Europe never broke up into rival power blocs, for example, liberal and monarchical, even when opportunities to do so presented themselves.[147] Instead, for a time the hegemons *pooled* their capabilities to facilitate collective continental management. Even after the Holy Alliance emerged as the political center of Europe, Britain never attempted to counter it by creating a liberal common security association with Spain, Portugal, and France. In short, Russia's and Britain's behavior was more consistent with the role of trustee than hegemon.

The success of the Congress of Vienna in establishing a stable international order that satisfied all the major powers and avoided the construction of antagonistic blocs met the conditions I articulated as evidence of a group identity. First, during most of the deliberations, the great powers did indeed act as partners rather than adversaries in the face of enormous political pressures. Second, there was a clear concept of a group interest among the participants, even as the individual powers continued to recognize their own national interests. Finally, the representatives approached the question of European reconstruction largely from European and great power perspectives.

4   *Constructing a Pan-Italian Community*

Both the concert system of great powers and the common security association of monarchs eventually broke down. For some political scientists and historians this was inevitable. Robert Jervis, for example, argues that concert systems decay over time, as memories of the great war fades and old animosities return.[1] A. J. P. Taylor focuses in particular on the rise of Prussian and French power, coupled with the decline in Austrian and Russian power, as the principle explanation for the political changes that occurred in Europe during the middle of the century.[2] Both these explanations suggest that conflict and rivalry are the natural state of affairs in international relations and that therefore the Concert of Europe and Holy Alliance were historical flukes.

Yet the breakdown of these transnational political communities did not produce a new balance of power system throughout the continent. On the contrary, in southern and central Europe two amalgamated security communities were created from a hodgepodge of competing, historically antagonistic states, resulting in the integration of Italy and Germany. Moreover, the Vienna system itself decayed primarily because domestic political actors challenged its underlying principles, not because of aggression by revisionist states. Once again, it was not war but social revolution that precipitated this challenge.

In 1848 revolution swept the continent. Unlike 1789, the revolutions of 1848 were widespread, touching every part of Europe except England and Russia. Beginning with the revolt in Naples, and shortly after in Paris, revolution spread to fifteen European capitals.[3] The uprisings were the culmination of a series of economic, social and political crises that had been developing over the decade. They were diverse and multifaceted and caused by a variety of factors. However as a *European* phenomenon they were not only domestic revolts against kings, princes, and emperors; they collectively represented a transnational uprising against the political order established by the Vienna treaties of 1815.[4] Above all, they challenged the legitimacy of the monarchic state, which had been the foundation for the Vienna system. This created the permissive condition that allowed for the formation of new transnational identities and the establishment of amalgamated security communities.

Amalgamated security communities are perhaps the greatest anomaly in a system of sovereign states. The voluntary cession of state sovereignty toward a new political center violates our most basic assumptions about international relations, the instincts for political survival and independence.[5] Unlike the creation of an empire, where independent units are conquered and absorbed into the center, political integration is a *synthesis* of the component units and the creation of an entirely new political community. It thus requires symbiosis among the units, a condition I defined in chapter 1 as a measure of a strong positive identity. Chapters 4 and 5 will examine the conditions under which a diverse set of independent political actors can build symbiotic relationships that transcend juridical boundaries. This chapter will focus on the transformation of the Italian state system.

Italy as a Historical Anomaly

If political integration is a theoretical anomaly, the integration of Italy is also a *historical* one. Ever since the emergence of independent states and principalities during the fifteenth century, the Italian peninsula was governed by a classic balance of power system. Following the Peace of Lodi in 1454, five states of relatively equal power emerged—Milan, Venice, Florence, Rome, and Naples. A century later Piedmont was created by the House of Savoy. Not only did the principalities regularly fight among themselves, they often allied with European great powers against each other, a classic balancing practice.

The reorganization of the peninsula by Napoleon did not change this situation. While he consolidated some states and absorbed others into his empire, after his defeat the Congress of Vienna recreated the original prewar borders and restored the traditional royal families to their thrones. With the restoration of the old political boundaries came the old rivalries. As Metternich correctly observed at the time, "If disorder broke out in Florence, the inhabitants of Pisa or Pistoria would take sides with the opposition because he hates Florence. And so it happens that Naples is resentful of Rome, Rome of Bolgna, Leghorn of Ancona and Milan of Venice."[6] The integration of Italy is thus a hard case for theories of cohesive community.

What, then, accounts for the dramatic transformation that occurred several decades later? Much of the literature on nation building in the nineteenth century focuses on modernization and economic development as the driving forces for uniting various segments of society into a modern centralized state.[7] Increases in social communication and the development of a middle class help to break down traditional loyalties such as tribal or regional ties. Specifically, the rising power of the middle classes within the Italian principalities could be said to have created a demand for an integrated economy that would be more efficient for economic expansion.[8] Although these are empirically valid theories for explaining state building within Europe in general, they do not apply to the Italian case.

While many of the Italian principalities participated in Europe's rapid economic and commercial growth after 1820, their economic development proceeded unevenly and at a slower pace than in most other parts of Europe.[9] The principalities were not particularly good models of modernizing and expanding economies. Moreover, even if economic expansion did produce an increasingly influential middle class, this does not explain why the middle classes would choose to integrate their states with others rather than build their own national economies. There is little evidence that the relevant actors that facilitated political integration responded to economic demands from domestic interests.[10] Most important, political integration *preceded* economic integration. Whatever economic motivations may have existed among some sectors of the various populations, each step toward integration was preceded by a political crisis.

Another common explanation for Italian integration rests with the "romantic nationalist" argument that unification was the fulfillment of centuries of primordial cultural or ethnic attachments.[11] Italy was a nation in waiting, kept apart by external forces and great power politics. However, Italian history did not leave a legacy that could account for a national or ethnic consciousness to develop in the nineteenth century. The peninsula and islands that we now know as Italy were originally the territories of the Hellenic, Carthaginian, Etruscan, and Roman peoples. For a time they were united—along with much of southern Europe and the Middle East—under the Roman Empire. However, ancient Rome was the capital of a nonethnic Mediterranean empire, not an Italian state; its legacy was not Italy but the Papacy.[12]

When "Italy" reappeared during the Renaissance, it was not as a single political unit but rather as a peninsula of city-states.[13] The Teutonic peoples predominated in the north and Greek peoples in the Basilicata and Puglie regions. Arab, Norman, and Spanish stock had left their marks in Sicily, while the old Italic and Etruscan peoples remained in Tuscany.[14] In fact, there was not even a common language to tie them together. Regional dialects were the dominant form of communication; beyond that, Latin was the most common language in Rome, French in Turin, and Spanish in Naples, Sicily, and Sardinia.[15] Thus the term *risorgimento* (literally, rebirth or reawakening) to describe the integration of Italy is somewhat misleading.[16]

Finally, some argue that political integration was the result of changes in the balance of power in southern Europe. Among the major changes that occurred in the mid-nineteenth century was in the relative capabilities of the great powers. France became stronger and, with the rise of Louis Napoleon, more aggressive, while Austria was weakened by domestic revolts in Vienna, Prague, Hungary, and Bohemia. This provided the Italian states with an external ally against a distracted hegemon. However, while this could account for the ability of the Italian states to integrate without external interference, it does not explain *why* the states would wish to do so in the first place. In fact, given the long history of rivalry and conflict on the peninsula, it is counterintuitive.

This is bolstered by the fact that *none* of the great powers wished to see the creation of an Italian national state. If no one benefited from integration, it is difficult to attribute integration to power politics between the great powers. Therefore, while the creation of the Italian *state* was facilitated by the weakening of Austria and the breakup of the Holy Alliance following the revolutions of 1848 and the Crimean War in 1856, the creation of the Italian *nation* required a more fundamental shift in the identities of the Italian principalities.

From another perspective, one may argue that integration was facilitated by an increase in *Piedmont's* relative capabilities and the rise of a new breed of modern politicians willing to manipulate both the international situation and nationalist aspirations to their own advantage.[17] In this case, integration can be explained by the ascension of Camillo Benso, Count of Cavour, and his attempt to extend Piedmontese hegemony over the peninsular.[18] This is the strongest challenge to the theories offered in this book and the empirical evidence below will help us to determine its explanatory power. The logic of this argument requires that, first, integration was Piedmont's preferred outcome; second, that it took steps to impose its hegemony on the principalities through the use of military force; and third, that the principalities formed an unsuccessful balancing coalition in an attempt to thwart Piedmont's power grab.

This chapter offers an alternative explanation. It argues that the political integration of Italy can best be understood by conceptualizing it as a process through which the principle actors created an amalgamated security community. Specifically, I suggest that the Northern Italian Kingdom was a type a cohesive security arrangement organized on the basis of a common good and a shared sense of self, giving its members a positive stake in building and maintaining internal relationships. Based on the theories outlined in chapter 2, I hypothesize that the two conditions required for the construction of an amalgamated security community on the Italian peninsula are a transnational identity that is grounded in a cosmopolitan rather than a parochial nationalism and a "reference other" that embodies this identity and around which the independent units can coalesce. Under these conditions juridical borders are no longer viewed as protections of autonomy but rather as impediments toward unity.

In contrasting these rival explanations, this chapter will examine the alternative possibilities for the organization of the peninsula, explain why one of them won out over the others, trace the process through which political integration occurred, and explore the changing relationships among the principalities.

Competing Identities and the Organization of the Peninsula

Under the Vienna system the Italian peninsula was divided into independent monarchic states, most of whom were tied to the other European powers through dynastic lineage. Lombardy-Venetia was a kingdom within the Austrian empire, the Kingdom of the Two Sicilies was ruled by Bourbon monarchs with ties to France, and Modena and Tuscany were ruled by archdukes with dynastic ties to the Hapsburgs. Only the Papal States, which were ruled by the pope, and Piedmont, which was ruled by the House of Savoy, were governed by monarchs without ties to a European family. From this hodgepodge of competing political units, there was no obvious model for how the peninsula would be organized, even if the great powers were to renounce their interest in its future.

The organization of Italy would depended upon the kind of state or states the political elites wanted to construct or maintain. On a more basic level, it also depended upon they type of authority that would be the focus of political loyalty among the relevant actors: dynastic, national, religious, or popular. Any one of these could have been accommodated within a balance of power system of independent states, but only pan-nationalism required a radical reorganization of the peninsula.

As a result, even as major social, economic, and political changes swept the continent, the transformation of the peninsula was not only not inevitable; until the 1850s it was extremely unlikely. During the 1830s and 1840s four possible scenarios were proposed, each reflecting a different focus of identification and loyalty: a peninsula of sovereign states, a Catholic federation under the rule of the pope, a republican national state within a continent of national states, and an autonomous pan-Italian state.

The most obvious and widely supported alternative until well into the 1850s was a balance of power system of sovereign states. Each of the principalities had a strong core of political elites with an interest in maintaining the status quo that had been established in Vienna. The "legitimist principle," which was the foundation of the Vienna system, had justified the restoration of the pre-Napoleonic ruling houses within the principalities. As long as the principalities continued to define themselves in dynastic terms, the Vienna settlement reflected the interests of the political elites. Monarchic solidarity tied the Italian states to the other monarchies of Europe, and the principles of Europeanism and great power management offered them a guarantee of their existing institutions. Under these conditions integration was never a possibility, since the accumulation of power in the hands of rulers over several generations inevitably produced dynastic interests that were at variance with those of the nation.

Austrian control of Lombardy and Venetia was not seen as a problem for the rest of the peninsula, since there was no perceived tie between those regions and the sovereign states of Italy. In fact, during this period many of the elites saw Austria as an ally in helping them to maintain their rule domestically and in balancing the power of the other principalities. Austria's influence over the Italian states was due not so much to the terms of the peace settlement or to Austrian military power, but rather to the fact that most Italian governments were even more conservative than Austria and thus sought Austria's help to protect the monarchy on the peninsula.[19] While the public did not welcome Austrian rule in Lombardy, the Austrian archdukes who ruled Modena and Tuscany were given warm welcomes by the people when they returned.[20]

Moreover, to the extent that nationalist feeling existed, it was of a provincial rather than a cosmopolitan type. This is captured well by Genovese delegate Pareto, who wrote a letter to Lord Castlereagh during the Congress of Vienna opposing a proposal to merge Piedmont with Genoa: "National spirit . . . certainly could not exist in the amalgamation of two peoples, Genoese and Piedmontese, divided by their character, their habits, and by an invincible antipathy. . . . Vain would be the attempt to make them one nation."[21] Consequently, throughout the Vienna period few Italians wished to form a unified state.[22] In fact, following his return to Piedmont, King Vittorio Emanuele—whose son would later lead a war of independence against Austria—set out to destroy every trace of "Italian" institutions, seeking in essence to de-Italianize his state.[23]

Vincenzo Gioberti's neo-Guelph movement promoted a second alternative: a transnational Catholic community to be centered within the Italian peninsula. To this end, the movement proposed uniting Italy into a federation of Catholic states under the rule of the pope. This reflected a widespread identification with Catholicism among the political elites and general population that cut across state boundaries. Gioberti was not proposing to build an Italian state with Catholicism as the official religion; rather, he advocated the construction of a worldwide center of Catholicism, a political base for the Vatican as a transnational actor. As he argued:

> The real principle of Italian unity . . . the Papacy, is supremely ours and our nation's because it created the nation and has been rooted here for eighteen centuries.[24]
>
> That the Pope is naturally, and should be effectively, the civil head of Italy is a truth forecast in the nature of things, confirmed by many centuries of history, recognized on past occasions by the peoples and princes of our land, and only thrown into doubt by those commentators who drank at foreign springs and diverted their poison to the motherland.[25]

In this sense the referent society was the Papal States. The idea of federation rather than integration was based on dual loyalties: one to the Catholic Italian nation and the other to the provincial state. This would have led to a structure somewhat analogous to that of the United States under the Articles of Confederation, which struck a cord with many politically conscious Italians who wanted to reconcile their desire for constitutional government and national unity with their strong Catholic faith. However, it would not only have required the Italian princes and ministers to reconcile their policies with those of the Church but also demanded that the Papal

States view themselves as part of a national political entity. In effect, church and state would merge, not merely work in coalition. It was the conflict between these two transnational identities—Catholicism and pan-Italianism—that ultimately eliminated this option as an alternative. The Papal States did not accept the tie between state and religion, and this created a conflict between national and religious loyalties.

A third alternative was to tie pan-nationalism to republicanism. This program was proposed by Giuseppe Mazzini, whose version of nationalism was based on national self-determination rather than cultural or ethnic autonomy.[26] Drawing from the philosophy of the French revolution, Mazzini identified the people with the nation; the people would reflect the will of the nation and vice versa. He argued that "the people have no existence where, owing to a forced union of races or families, there is no unity of belief and moral purpose; these factors alone constitute nations."[27] This conception of the nation inevitably sees the people—and the nation—as something separate from the state. This was a form of secular (or civic) nationalism in which popular rule would replace monarchic rule.

Unlike Gioberti and the advocates of an Italian kingdom, Mazzini's vision was also pan-Europeanist in that he saw not only an Italian nation but a Europe comprised of republican national states. In addition to the construction of an Italian state, he envisioned a United States of Europe, toward which his Italian nation might lead the way.[28] To this end, he instigated not only the formation of the pan-nationalist organization Young Italy, but also encouraged the formation of Young France, Young Germany, Young Poland, Young Switzerland, and ultimately Young Europe. Young Europe was conceived as a counterhegemonic coalition to the Holy Alliance, a union of free nations against the alliance of dynastic states. Thus this understanding of "Italy" was tied to the development of a broader European community of national states.

In contrast to the neo-Guelphist concept of a dual transnational community based on church and nation, Mazzini's idea was a dualism based on a pan-Italian nation and a cosmopolitan Europe. Mazzini believed that just as the French revolution had freed the individual, the Italian revolution would free the nation.[29] In this sense the republican's reference group was France and the French concept of nationalism. Mazzini's link between the Italian nation and the European community suggests that the transnational concepts of Europeanism and pan-Italianism were not necessarily in conflict, given the proper conditions. It was at least theoretically possible to simultaneously identify with *both* the European community and one's own pan-national community. Had this form of nationalism dominated in Italy and Germany, history may have taken a radically different turn in the twentieth century.

Finally, another form of pan-nationalism emerged, which advocated the construction of a cohesive national state that would eventually develop into a major power. As an autonomous power in its own right, it would owe little to Europe or to the universalistic idea of Europeanism. Rather its legitimation would derive from those special and unique characteristics that would make Italy great. This view was best represented by the National Society, which was formed by Piedmontese intellectuals in 1858. For the leaders of the National Society the nation was closely linked to the state as an institution:

> To recover the prosperity and glory she knew in the Middle Ages, Italy must become not only independent but politically united. Everything points irresistibly to political unification. . . . Science, industry, commerce and the arts all need it. . . . The spirit of the age is moving toward concentration, and woe betide any nation that holds back!
>
> What use is it to have invented the compass, to have discovered the New World . . . to have given birth to Caesar and Bonaparte[30] if a foreign ruler can order Neapolitans to fight Romans and can enlist Tuscans, Lombards and Venetians to fight alongside the Croats in his own army?[31]

This merger of nationalism with raison d'état saw state-building and nation-building as co-dependent. It was this legacy, not that of Mazzini, Gioberti, or Garibaldi, that provided the ideological basis for Mussolini's twentieth-century form of Italian nationalism.

This alternative, which eventually was adopted by the leaders of the northern and central states, promoted Piedmont as the referent society that epitomized not only the Italian nation but also the future Italian state. In fact, it was not Piedmont's military power that made it into a positive reference group for those advocating this form of pan-nationalism. Rather, it was its image as a progressive, modern, and efficient state that could best represent the glory of Italy. Following the revolutions of 1848, Piedmont emerged as a model constitutional state with a strong efficient administration, rapidly expanding economy, progressive education, and liberal social policies.[32]

What explains the eventual triumph of this last alternative? In many ways it was the process through which integration occurred, that is, as an amalgamated security community rather than through economic interdependence, a nationalist uprising, a cultural revolution, or a religious crusade. Leading up to the rapid series of events that changed the political map of southern Europe, the transnationalist Italian identity evolved from a common relationship to the rest of Europe, the activities of transnational organizations, and the rise of Piedmont as a referent society. All this was facilitated by a common experience of high intensity and long duration, the wars against Austria. The next sections will examine these in more detail.

A Common Relationship to Europe

One of the factors that helped to facilitate the development of a common transnational Italian consciousness was its external treatment first by Napoleon and then by the great powers of Europe. For almost three quarters of a century the Italian principalities shared a unique common relationship to the rest of Europe. Although neither Napoleon nor the great powers wished to create a unified Italian state, both treated the Italian principalities as a single political entity. This was done primarily for administrative convenience. Rather than approaching each state as an autonomous sovereign unit—as was done with the other secondary states of Europe such as Spain or Belgium—both the French Empire and the Vienna settlement considered the individual states to be part of a broader "Italian question."[33] These perceptions were ultimately projected onto the Italian states, making the concept of Italy as a political idea not only thinkable, but a focus of discussion by the European community.

Napoleon had divided the peninsula into three parts by abolishing the separate principalities, states, and republics. The northeastern regions were organized into the Kingdom of Italy, the southern areas into the Kingdom of Naples, and the remaining units—Piedmont, Genoa, the Papal States, and Tuscany—were annexed to France. This reorganization, together with the introduction of a uniform code of laws, a common language of administration (Tuscan), and system of government, had a great impact on the political thought of the Italian people.[34] For the first time since the Roman Empire, there was some commonalty among what had been a hodgepodge of political units. Stuart Woolf adds that the rationalization of Italy by Napoleon was the first step toward creating a unified state.[35]

After the defeat of Napoleon the great powers reestablished the original juridical borders with a few minor changes. However, the Italian principalities as a group were treated differently than the other European monarchies. Unlike the settlement for the rest of Europe, the peninsula was placed under foreign influence, primarily Austrian. Moreover, while the legitimist principle had enabled the Italian royal families to reclaim their positions within the principalities, they were excluded from the club of European monarchies that had formed among the great powers.

Had Napoleon and the Congress of Vienna established strong independent Italian monarchies, the political basis for a unified Italian nation would have likely been missing.[36] By keeping the Italian states weak and under great power tutelage, the great powers helped to prevent the development of strong state institutions and loyalties among the rulers, elites, and population.[37] Thus, when dynastic legitimacy ultimately collapsed in the 1850s, the new authorities could not simply assume the machinery of the state as had been done in much of Europe. The state *was* the monarchy and without the latter the former did not have a strong independent existence. This limited the extent to which political elites could develop strong loyalties to the state.

Consequently, in an ironic twist, the Vienna system itself helped contribute toward the eventual development of a transnational identity among the Italian states. In designating Austria as the sole great power responsible for maintaining security and overseeing Italy's economic development, the Congress of Vienna isolated the peninsula from the rest of Europe. In short, it made the peninsula politically, economically, and militarily impenetrable. Thus, a unique relationship developed among the Italian states, that of object rather than participant in Europe. In other words, while the other secondary powers such as Spain, Holland, and Portugal were treated as important parts of the Vienna system, the Italian states became *objects* for securing a European equilibrium. The self-other distinction that is often the basis for nationalist identification was in part *created* by the congress.

Transnational Organizations and Transnational Identities

Another factor influencing the development of a transnational consciousness was the exclusive nature of interaction between domestic political actors within the principalities. These interactions were facilitated by transnational organizations. From 1839 through 1847 scientific congresses were held annually in Pisa, Turin, Florence, Padna, Lucca, Milan, Naples, Genoa, and Venice. These gatherings brought together scientists and naturalists from every principality. While they were largely scientific in nature, in the words of historian Bolton King, it became "impossible for Italians of different states to come together without giving something of a national complexion to their meetings."[38] That is, since only people from the Italian states attended, the congresses were defined partly by their Italian particularism. Economic questions led to discussions of a customs union, social problems led to discussions of politics, and geographic issues brought out discussions of the future of the peninsula.

Beginning in 1844 the congresses began to elect committees of members representing various Italian states to study such common problems as elementary education, the search for coal deposits, the silk industry, the reintroduction of a uniform metric system, steam power, and deficiency diseases.[39] Besides facilitating cooperative relationships among the principalities on educational, economic, and scientific matters, the congresses forged a new cultural unity in the peninsula, testifying to the economic and intellectual interdependence of its states.[40] It is important to note that the congresses were not initiated by nationalists hoping to nurture an Italian consciousness but by political elites seeking to further their scientific and economic development. Thus the process of cooperation led to more cohesive relationships between traditional rivals.

In another sense the congresses broke down some of the regional barriers that had led most Italians to view themselves from the vantage point of their sovereign states rather than as a conceptual whole. Leopold II of Tuscany, one of the early sponsors of the congresses, brought in scientists and educators from throughout the peninsula, appointing them to important educational and cultural posts in his state.[41] This helped to "Italianize" the scientific and educational institutions.

The principalities also began to cooperate economically. In 1847 Piedmont, Tuscany, and the Papal States signed a treaty forming a customs union, forging a unique form of cooperation (although not economic integration) among the three states from the northern and central regions of Italy. In addition, the government of Piedmont began to build rail lines from Turin to other Italian cities. A short line from Naples to Porticic was opened in 1839 and another was built a year later, which ran from Milan to Monaza. During the 1840s the pace of rail construction across the peninsula increased considerably. For the first time there was some semblance of a geographic, if not political, union. As Piedmontese nobleman Massino D'Azeglio noted, the railways would "stitch the boot" of the Italian peninsula.[42]

Obviously, convening interstate congresses and building rail lines across sovereign borders in and of themselves do not create a transnational community. Rather it was the *exclusivity* of these practices that fostered perceptions of a positive interdependence that was limited to the Italian states.

Perhaps the most important factor in building transnational relationships within the peninsula was the various networks of democratic activists that helped to create a transnational consciousness among the educated and elite classes. These networks played an important role in deemphasizing the juridical divisions among the Italian states in favor of ideological solidarity. As one historian argues, the activists created among themselves a special sense of group solidarity that was built upon a shared intellectual heritage and a common ideology.[43] Democratic movements had existed in every major city within the peninsula since the early 1830s, although until the mid-1940s they tended to remain secretive and isolated from each other. Most of these movements had the dual goal of expelling the Austrians from their respective states and establishing constitutional systems of government within them. Many also sought to curb the spiritual and ideological power of the Church, and some promoted Italian unity.

During the period surrounding the 1848 revolutions, activists within local and regional movements began to make more formal contacts with similar activists in other regions and states.[44] The flow of volunteers from throughout the peninsula to help Piedmont in its war against Austria in 1949 (which I discuss below) further developed this network. All this culminated in widespread participation in the Lombard Campaign (against Austria), the Five Days in Milan (the Venetian revolution), and the proclamation of the Roman republic following an insurrection in the Papal States. While these revolutions were eventually defeated, the experiments helped to strengthen the movements for independence and democracy. This would have lasting effects. Spencer Di Scala estimates that following the defeat of the 1848 revolutions as many as fifty thousand exiles from these movements migrated to Piedmont.[45] Once there, many decided to place independence and unity above republicanism as their immediate goals and helped to influence Piedmontese policy (particularly that of Cavour) concerning Italy. In sum, as the democratic activists began to *act* together as Italians, their thinking and perceptions became more cosmopolitan. This had an important impact on the future political elites in the northern and central regions.

A Common Experience: War and Unity in 1849

Ultimately it was a common experience that convinced the politically active population that they were Italians as much as they were Piedmontese, Tuscans, and Napalese: the fight against their newly constituted negative reference group, Austria. Until the 1840s there was little resistance to Austrian domination of the northeastern and central peninsula. As argued above, Austria's presence on the peninsula served the interests of the reigning elites. This changed in 1848. Accompanying the uprisings that began to spread throughout Europe, revolutions occurred in every Italian state except Piedmont. The principle aim of most of the revolutionary movements in Italy was to acquire a constitution for each state and to see that it was respected.[46] Dynastic rulers were driven out of the northern Italian states, the Bourbons were expelled from the Kingdom of Two Sicilies, and the pope and his government was expelled from the Papal States. A Roman republic was declared. While the revolutions were later defeated by Austrian and French troops, the legitimacy of the Italian princes was badly undermined and their dynastic rights were no longer respected.

The 1848 revolutions in Lombardy and Venetia were directed mostly against Austrian rule, and this ultimately brought the Italian nation into conflict with the Hapsburgs for the first time. Tension had been building since 1847 when local political leaders in Milan instigated a boycott of Austrian tobacco. Austrian troops responded by blowing tobacco smoke in the faces of the Venetians and forcing them to smoke Austrian cigars. While the "tobacco riots" that followed failed to dislodge the Austrian administration, the Lombards got their chance a year later. Taking advantage of domestic unrest in Austria, revolutionaries overthrew the local administration and temporarily drove Austrian security forces out of Milan. The provisional government voted for union—rather than alliance—with Piedmont without any prior indication from the latter that they would join the Lombardian opposition against Austria.

In fact, if history was any guide, Piedmont should have been expected to *aid* Austria in its war against Milan, which would have helped the Piedmontese to maintain their hegemony in the region. However, this time the Venetians appealed to Piedmont for support in the name of Italian solidarity, forcing King Carlo Alberto to choose between his conflicting roles as head of the House of Savoy (whose interest lay with an Austrian alliance) and leader of an Italian state. The rapidly changing political situation forced Alberto to reevaluate his position. The decision of the king to take up the Lombard's cause was the first indication that Piedmont would shift its loyalty from dynasticism to the defense of a fellow Italian state. This required a reconception of Piedmontese identity in transnational terms.

Before this Carlo Alberto had seen Piedmont as a state of its own, not to be submerged in a union of other Italian states.[47] There is no evidence that Piedmont's actions were motivated by a desire to expand within the northern peninsula. Nor was Austria a threat to the Piedmontese. Venetia was legally part of the Austrian Empire, an arrangement that had continued for more than three decades. Balance of power and territorial considerations did not appear to be a factor. Thus, while the 1848 revolution in Vienna may have provided the *means* for Piedmont to challenge Austrian authority, it did not provide the motivation. Moreover, since Piedmont did not face a revolutionary challenge itself, Alberto was not acting to save his throne. Rather, the revolutions throughout Italy had a significant effect on his understanding of Piedmont vis-à-vis the other Italian states. This understanding was reflected in future prime minister Cavour's statement to Carlo Alberto prior to Piedmont's entrance into the war, printed in the newly formed Italian newspaper, *Il Risorgimento*: "The *nation* is at war with Austria already. The whole nation is rushing to the succor of the Lombards, the volunteers have crossed the frontiers, *our fellow citizens* are openly making munitions and sending them to the Milanese."[48] Alberto's response is also illustrative of his changing understandings:

> We, out of love for our common race, understanding as we do what is now happening, and supported by public opinion, hasten to associate ourselves with the unanimous admiration which Italy bestows upon you. Peoples of Lombardy and Venetia . . . we are now coming to offer you in the latter phases of your fight the help which a brother expects from a brother.[49]

This change can be largely explained by the evolution of Piedmont from a dynastic state to a national one. This changed its relationship to the other principalities and created a new role as a referent society for pan-Italianism. As argued in chapter 2, roles are formed within social settings, always in relation to others.[50] This concept of roles is key to explaining Piedmont's behavior in the integration process. As a dynastic state representing the House of Savoy, Piedmont traditionally viewed its interest as an ally of Austria against other Italian principalities. Since his accession in 1831, Carlo Alberto had seen Austria as an principle ally in the legitimist cause.[51] The Piedmontese army had been trained to fight for the dynasty and the Holy Alliance side by side with Austria.[52] However, as Piedmont's elites began to view their country as an Italian state, Austria became an enemy dominating a fellow Italian state.

Several points are illustrative in understanding how Piedmont's identification with pan-Italiansim influenced its perceptions of interest. First, the

Piedmontese were woefully unprepared for war, suggesting that the decision to enter was not preplanned.[53] Militarily it was not a wise decision. However, Piedmont's interests did not appear to be either dynastic expansion or territorial aggrandizement. Rather, in the words of Cavour, "The moral effect of an opening of hostilities and the relief of Milan would be of more use to the Italian cause than the defeat of a body of five hundred men would injure it."[54]

Second, at a crucial point, instead of concentrating on fighting the war, Carlo Alberto insisted on holding plebiscites in both Lombardy and Venetia on whether they wished to merge with Piedmont, even though its leadership had already voted to do so. This move was criticized as a major military blunder by contemporaries and historians alike.[55] While holding plebiscites in the middle of a war made little sense from a military point of view, it was crucial if Piedmont was serious about building a North Italian Kingdom whose authority was based on national sovereignty. This required the legitimation of the population.

Third, even after the Italian alliance was defeated in late 1848 Carlo Alberto resumed the war against Austria in 1849—after the emperor suppressed the Austrian revolution and rebuilt the Austrian army—largely because he was committed to the independence of northern Italy. His resumption of the war was on behalf of Italy, not Piedmont.[56] From a purely Piedmontese perspective resuming the war on behalf of Lombardy made little sense. However, from an Italian perspective it was a war of national liberation. To be an Italian meant he had to act like one.

After the peace agreement was signed, Austria offered to give Piedmont the principality of Parma and a waiver of indemnity if it would modify its constitution and reestablish the Piedmontese-Austrian alliance. King Vittorio Emanuele, Carlo Alberto's son, who assumed the throne after upon his father's abdication, refused, saying, "I will hold the tricolor (the symbol of the Italian nation) high and firm."[57] Although cabinet minister Gioberti proposed that Piedmont send troops into Tuscany to restore order after the republicans took power, both the king and his cabinet refused, arguing that they could not send Italians to fight Italians. This was a radical departure from the diplomatic history of the Italian state system.

The wars of 1848 and 1849 demonstrate several other points about the development of a transnational identity among the sovereign states of Italy. First, before the revolutions and war, Piedmont did not see itself as an Italian state. It was only through its participation in the war of independence on behalf of another state—a common experience—that it developed the notion that the war was an Italian one. This presents a good example of how *process* and interaction can create new identities. Second, and somewhat related to the first point, the war against Austria was not aimed at building a united Italian nation. It was purely anti-Austrian, focused on achieving independence for the two northern states. However, once the war took on a national character, it changed the perceptions of those participating. Mead's "community of attitudes" had been formed, providing a framework from which the political leaders could evaluate the appropriate ways of responding to the situation.

Third, the revolutions and the war discredited the Italian princes in the central Italian states and, further, discredited the pope as a national political force. Both the grand duke of Tuscany and the pope had to be restored with the aid of foreign forces.[58] Moreover, the pope's refusal to support the war against Austria at the crucial moment forever discredited him and the Papacy as a force for national leadership. The pope had argued, logically from a Catholic perspective, that he could not sanction a war of one Catholic country against another. The 1848 events therefore demonstrated that no matter how sympathetic the pope might be to the Italian nation, this would always be subordinated to his role as transnational leader of the Catholic world. He would even conceivably call in foreign powers to intervene on his behalf.[59] His stand forced political leaders to choose between Catholicism and Italianism, and almost all chose the latter.

At the same time, with the defeat of the Roman republic and the Venetian revolution — both showcases for Italian republicanism — Mazzini's approach to Italian nationalism was no longer tenable. The decision by France to send in troops to forcibly reinstall the pope discredited the idea of a United States of Europe comprised of republican national states. The Romans had assumed that France, the "mother of all republics," would back the republican cause rather than the papal institutions.[60] They failed to understand the France itself was conflicted between its role as a liberator (under the new revolutionary government) and as a Catholic state. Even as Louis Napoleon's troops entered the city, the French could not decide whether to act as good Catholics and restore the pope or behave as good republicans and protect the republic.[61] The June elections brought in a majority of pro-clerical deputies, and this decided the issue. Ultimately, the perceived sellout by France and the refusal of Great Britain to lend its support to the national and constitutional cause made any identification with Europeanism unlikely.

Vittorio Emanuele's strong support for the other principalities in his negotiations with Austria highlighted the special relationship that existed

among the Italian states and confirmed the House of Savoy as the acknowledged leader of Italy. The final result of the war was thus to increase the
prestige of Piedmont, a phenomenon that would have been unthinkable in
almost any previous period in the history of the peninsula. In the years prior
to 1848–1849 Piedmont had been regarded as a dangerous rival. In fact,
previous attempts by other Italian states to involve Austria in a defensive
league derived largely from anxiety of Piedmont.[62] The change in the per-
ception of Piedmont can be explained by the fact that the other Italian states
had begun to think of themselves as Italians, in which case Piedmont was
no longer a dangerous adversary but a leader of a pan-Italian community.

In sociological terms, Piedmont became a positive reference group that
embodied the transnational Italian identity. This feeling was articulated by
Tucson leader Bettino Ricasoli, who stated, "I want to make Tuscany a
province of Piedmont, for that is the only way for her to become a province
of Italy.[63] And in Milan, where animosity and suspicion toward Piedmont
had traditionally been strong, the members of the government's peace commission wrote: "Despite our losses, the foundations of free and independent
Italy still stand firm in Piedmont, that when conditions of Europe permit us
to claim the rights of our common nationality, all Italy may turn to her, as
the natural champion of this cause.[64]

The identification of Piedmont with Italy was particularly appealing to
the liberals and republicans who would later assume power in the central
principalities. Piedmont was the only state on the peninsula to emerge from
the 1848 revolutions and the Austrian war with its constitution intact.[65] Its
steadfast defense of the constitution against the wishes of Austria lifted Piedmont to first claim on liberal Italy's hope and gratitude. [66] The constitution
guaranteed basic political and civil rights and established a parliament, a
goal sought by most of the democrats. For the liberals, Piedmont was thus
seen as a model state to be emulated.

The Creation of an Italian Security Community

The integration of the peninsula ultimately required all the sovereign
states to cede much of their sovereignty to an abstract concept, Italy. In
practical terms, this meant merger with Piedmont. The creation of Italy
occurred in four stages, beginning with the construction of an amalgamated
security community between the northern and central Italian states. This
was a direct outgrowth of fighting together as a single unit against Austria in
1859.

During the summer of that year, Piedmont conspired with France to provoke a war with Austria, hoping to expel the latter from the peninsula. According to the secret agreement, France would support the merger of Lombardy and Venetia with Piedmont into a Kingdom of North Italy, as originally proposed during the 1849 war, and, in return, Piedmont would cede Nice and Savoy to France. With the support of France secured, the Piedmontese leaders reached out to their historical rivals in the name of pan-Italianism. Speaking in terms of a transnational Italian community, Vittorio Emanuele made his famous "cry of anguish" speech to parliament calling for all Italians to fight as one against Austria. Thousands of volunteers from each of the northern and central principalities responded by joining Piedmont's efforts on behalf of Italy.

The war was short and inconclusive, ending with an armistice between France and Austria. Echoing a time-honored tradition, the two great powers sought to settle the "Italian question" between themselves; Piedmont was excluded from the negotiations. This enabled France to sell out Piedmont by agreeing to allow Venetia to remain within the Austrian sphere. This time, however, the situation was different. The participation of volunteers from throughout the peninsula under the command of Piedmont blurred the conceptual boundaries that had previously divided the states and created a new type of security arrangement. The disparate states were not military allies but symbiotic partners. Therefore the agreement would have been impossible to enforce without the force of arms directed against the entire peninsula.[67]

This became clear when revolutionaries overthrew the ruling monarchs in Tuscany, Parma, and Modena. The revolutions were not initially nationalist; they were aimed at toppling discredited dynasties kept in power by Austria.[68] However, immediately following the insurrections, the political leaders of these states each announced their interest in joining the Piedmont-Lombardy union, much to the disapproval of France.[69] The French-Austrian agreement had called for restoring the dispossessed princes in the central duchies; however, Parma and Tuscany refused to go along with this agreement and announced their union with Piedmont. Their interest in creating this amalgamated security community was a recognition that they shared a positive interdependence and thus their fortunes would rise and fall together. This recognition was strengthened by their common relationship to the European great powers.

The rulers of these duchies then set out to "Piedmontize" their states by unifying their currencies, customs, and postal arrangements.[70] They pledged their loyalty to Vittorio Emanuele, in effect ceding their sovereignty to a foreign king. As pro-unionist Tabarrini argued after Florence requested annexation, "Either the Florentines do not know what they are doing or if they do, they are giving the greatest possible proof of self-sacrifice for Italy. . . . The Florentines are committing political suicide."[71] As a result, Tuscany decided in favor of transnational solidarity over autonomy. Tuscany's decision was followed by a series of plebiscites in the central Italian duchies in 1860. Elite and popular support for these initiatives was largely the result of the participation of the central Italian rulers in the National Society, which at the time did not foresee a united Italy.[72] Working within the National Society, however, they developed a pan-Italian identity over time. The nature of their association influenced their understanding of self and interest.

Even at this point Piedmont was unsure whether it wanted to merge with the states of central Italy, as this would have meant the end of the House of Savoy as a political entity. For the monarchy, questions of identity were as important than those of territory. Before the war Cavour had not intended to annex Tuscany; rather he preferred an independent Central Italy as an ally against Austria.[73] Thus Piedmont at first hesitated to accept annexation of the central duchies. However, as Cavour continued to modernize Piedmont and identify its interests more closely with Italian aspirations strong domestic pressure grew for the creation of an Italian state.[74] Despite other political considerations to the contrary, Piedmont could not deny an Italian state entry into its newly formed security community. To do so would have undermined its role as a leader of the Italian nation. The new Italian parliament responded by voting to approve annexation by means of plebiscite of any Italian territory that wished to be part of Italy. The link between the House of Savoy and Piedmont had ended.

The creation of an amalgamated security community between the northern and central states formed the core of the new Italian state. The complete integration of the peninsula, however, ultimately required the overthrow of two competing traditional authorities, dynastic and papal, in the southern peninsula. Both actions were the result of revolution and war. The incorporation of Naples and Sicily into the new Italian nation was facilitated by Italian nationalist Giuseppe Garibaldi's "march of the thousand," following the overthrow of the Bourbon monarchy in the Kingdom of Two Sicilies. While Cavour preferred to limit the new nation to the northern and central regions for political and administrative reasons, Garibaldi's success in defeating the Bourbons in Sicily and Naples created a new climate of pan-nationalism in the north.[75] Both king and cabinet ultimately supported the expedition and agreed to sponsor plebiscites in both states. Given that the political elites supported integration, the outcome of the plebiscites was never in doubt, although the fairness of the voting was highly suspect.

Garibaldi's mission had sparked enthusiasm within the cabinet to complete the direct line between north and south. Cavour thereby sent the Piedmontese army south to challenge the pope's temporal power, something that would have been a highly dangerous political move even a few years earlier. However, the political elites had already placed their futures with the pan-nationalist security community and therefore their religious loyalties became subordinated to their national ones. Within a few weeks the Papal States were conquered and, following the positive vote in the plebiscites, all but the city of Rome became part of Italy.

By 1860 it was obvious that the Italian states would have to make a final choice between the national and the Catholic ideal.[76] The total unity of the peninsula would require that the Papacy—which still reigned in Rome—be reconceptualized as a foreign power. Thus, while the Italian leaders maintained their spiritual loyalty to the Church, they would have to renounce the temporal power of the Pope. This would in effect end a thousand years of loyalty to Papal power. By 1861, however, identification with Italy had overshadowed loyalty to the Church. This attitude was articulated by Italian minister Baron Bettino Ricasoli, who said, "Europe must recognize that Rome was Italian, not a feud of the Catholic world."[77] Only the presence of French troops prevented Rome from joining the new Italian state. This obstacle was removed after the Franco-Prussian War of 1870 forced the removal of these troops and Rome became a part of Italy.

In 1861 the Italian parliament met in Turin and Vittorio Emanuele was crowned king of Italy "by the grace of God and the will of the nation," a recognition that his legitimation would now be based on pan-nationalist principles.[78] Thus, although there was some opposition to maintaining the title of Vittorio Emanuele II, sovereign authority was transferred from dynasty to nation. The interests of the king would no longer be defined by his role as head of the House of Savoy and leader of Piedmont but by the requirements of leading the new Italian nation. This was symbolically confirmed once the peninsula was finally fully unified in 1870, as the nation's capital was moved from Turin—the historic center of Piedmont—to Rome—the mythic center of the Italian nation. This marked the final transfer of power from the House of Savoy to the nation of Italy.

This chapter suggests the interests of the principalities were largely framed by the type of states they wished to form, indicating that the identity of the units are indeed relevant in determining the type of security arrangement that develops within a region. Historic rivalries and distrust were overcome only after the principalities reconceptualized themselves as Italians rather than as simply Tuscans, Parmans, or Piedmontese. Until this occurred, none of the political elites saw integration to be in their interest. Most historians agree that neither Vittorio Emanuele nor Cavour appeared to be motivated by primarily expansionist aims.[79] In fact, on seeing the problems that Naples could potentially cause for an integrated Italy, Cavour lamented the day that Garibaldi compelled him to annex that state.[80]

The domination of transnational over parochial identities among the Italian principalities came about through the unique relationship shared by the principalities, the activities by transnational actors, and a change in the types of states that populated the peninsula. It was facilitated by their common experiences during the wars of liberation and the 1848 revolutions. The revolutions of 1848 and 1859 provided the permissive cause by undermining the political foundation of dynastic authority within the principalities. The peninsula's status as a protectorate of the great powers, in particular Austria, helped to create a consciousness among the states that they shared a unique relationship vis-à-vis Europe. This, coupled with functional cooperation on economic, military, and technical matters, helped to facilitate the development of a common identity. Once Piedmont was seen as the embodiment of Italy's aspirations, it changed from a dangerous rival to a trusted ally.

Power and interest explanations cannot account for the political integration of the seven independent states into a new political community. While the integration of Italy may have been aided by power politics among the great powers (particularly France and Austria), it was not the cause. At the same time, using the standards of evidence articulated at the beginning of the chapter, we must reject a Piedmontese hegemony explanation. Integration was not Piedmont's preferred outcome until the other Italian states virtually forced it upon them. Nor did it attempt to impose its hegemony on the principalities through the use of military force. As a result, the principalities never attempted to form a balancing coalition in an attempt to thwart Piedmont's alleged power grab. Quite the contrary, in the case of the central and northern states the political elites *requested* annexation, and in the case of the south the general population supported it.

In sum, this chapter demonstrates that the integration of Italy was brought about through the construction of an amalgamated security community in the northern peninsula. This was facilitated by the development of a transnational identity that was grounded in a cosmopolitan rather than a parochial nationalism. It was further facilitated through the creation of a reference other—Piedmont—that embodied this identity and provided a center around which the independent units could coalesce. Under these conditions juridical borders were no longer viewed as a protection of autonomy but rather as impediments toward unity. In a broader sense, it also demonstrates that nationalism is not necessarily a divisive force focused on parochial identities but can be a unifying agent seeking to construct a political community that cuts across juridical borders.

5   *Constructing a Pan-Germanic Community*

In the last chapter I examined the conditions under which specific forms of interaction among independent states can lead to a symbiotic relationship that diminishes the conceptual boundaries dividing them. In this chapter I will shift the emphasis from external interactions to the internal dynamics *within* the interacting states. This will enable us to more closely examine the role of domestic politics in changing the way political elites construct boundaries between societies.

Germany Integration as a Historical Anomaly

Like the integration of Italy, the creation of Germany was neither natural nor inevitable. For a millennium the Germanic regions of Europe had been a collection of medieval fiefdoms, Holy Roman electorates, petty principalities, and dynastic houses. While the idea of a Germanic culture had existed since the Middle Ages, the concept of Germany as a political community encompassing multiple principalities did not emerge until the 1840s.[1] In fact, from the time that the idea of a German *Reich* was conceived in the tenth century, political authorities had expended far more energy maintaining the principalities and ecclesiastical territories *independent* of the Reich than developing the Reich itself.[2]

Moreover, history did not even leave a definitive geographical legacy upon which to build a German territorial state. The settlements of the Germanic peoples fluctuated considerably in the thousand years prior to integration. There were no clear landmarks or boundaries that marked German territory.[3] Instead, the political organization of central Europe can be traced to the Holy Roman Empire, an ecclesiastical conglomeration of electorates, principalities, and dynastic houses. Created in the tenth century by Otto I (a Saxon king), the empire included the former Roman parts of central Europe and much of Charlemagne's Carolinginan Empire.

In 1438 Albrecht II of the House of Hapsburg succeeded to the throne of the empire and, with the exception of a three-year interlude, the Hapsburgs held the emperorship until it was dissolved by Napoleon in 1806. The Hapsburgs slowly expanded the empire well beyond what could be considered the Germanic regions into the areas now known as Hungary, Bohemia, and Italy. While this was partly accomplished through war, the primary mechanism for territorial expansion was dynastic marriage.[4] This is the origin of Austria's multiethnic empire. Until the rise of the national state there was nothing paradoxical about the Hapsburgs ruling over both German and non-German lands. The political and social foundation of the Holy Roman Empire was not ethnic or cultural community but Christian universalism. The empire was considered the guardian of Christian civilization and inherited what the Roman Church had preserved of classical antiquity. Although it was referred to as the Holy Roman Empire of the German Nation, German-speaking people were a minority.

The Protestant Reformation in the sixteenth century caused a major split in the unity of the empire. This laid the foundation for what would become two central European political traditions, Catholic and Protestant, ultimately represented by Austria and Prussia. The main beneficiary of the split was the House of Hohenzollern, which ruled the Holy Roman electorate of Brandenburg. Brandenberg had been a small weak electorate, heavily populated by the eastern Slavs.[5] This changed when the Hohenzollerns joined the central European revolt against the Papacy by siding with the Lutherans. Its role as a leader in the Protestant movement elevated its power and status throughout Protestant central Europe. It soon expanded through the acquisition of three small territories in the western part of what is now known as Germany. The new entity become known as Brandenberg-Prussia, a dynastic state headed by the House of Hohenzollern. With the Treaty of Augsburg in 1555, a stable balance of power system grew within central Europe.

Why, then, was a German nation-state created in the late nineteenth century, and why did it take the form that it did? More important, what made the rulers, revolutionaries, and political classes think of themselves as Germans rather than Prussians, Badans, and Bavarians? While some authors attribute this to the power of German nationalism, most modern historians reject the romantic nationalist explanation.[6] Instead, most political scientists and historians tend to view German integration as the result of a hegemonic struggle between Austria and Prussia for control of central Europe.[7] As such, the focus is largely on the person of Otto von Bismarck, master of realpolitik and symbol of Prussian power.[8] As in the case of the Italian Cavour, Bismarck is seen to represent a generation of European political leaders who sought to expand state power through bureaucratic efficiency and the manipulation of nationalist movements.

This explanation is powerful but highly insufficient for several reasons. First, although Bismarck certainly played a key role in the creation of Germany, the process that led to German integration began well before to his appointment as minister-president in 1862. Moreover, while Bismarck's policies were based primarily on Prussian interests, these interests expanded considerably during his tenure. As historian Louis Snyder argues, the transformation of Bismarck from narrow *Prussian* to broader *German* nationalism is one of the most important factors in the history of nineteenth-century Europe.[9] A Bismarck-centric explanation would have to account for this change.

Second, the power-and-interests approach would have to take into account the divisions among the ruling elites. Bismarck was influential, but he was still only one of a number of political actors within Prussia. Most Prussian officials, including Bismarck himself, *opposed* the creation of a German state, and the king was averse to ceding Hohenzollern rule to a national state. There were at least three political forces within Prussia, each with a different vision for the future of their country: the Hohenzollern monarchy, the Prussian bureaucratic state, and the German cultural nation. Explanations based on raison d'état do not account for how these competing interests were reconciled. Even within the German principalities there was an ongoing conflict between particularism and pan-nationalism, making it difficult speak in terms of a single state interest.

Finally, realist explanations assume that Austria and Prussia were struggling for similar ends, to dominate central Europe through territorial expansion. However, the raisons d'état of Austria and Prussia depended less upon some abstract notion of state power and more on the type of state each wished to become. During the period under investigation Prussia, Austria, and the German principalities were each undergoing profound internal changes brought about by the revolutions of 1848. Their interests ultimately depended upon how they resolved this question of state identity. While Austria wished to remain a multinational empire, Prussia was internally divided over whether it wished to be a national or dynastic state. Both of their preferred outcomes depended upon the resolution of these issues.

Consequently, this chapter argues that neither the romantic nationalist nor the power-and-interests explanations are sufficient. While German nationalism did help to cultivate a transnational German identity among the political actors in Prussia and the German principalities, the creation of Germany was ultimately a political process involving competing definitions of the German nation. It required a prior construction of an amalgamated security community in central Europe, an arrangement that equated the security of the principalities with that of the German nation.

Developing a Common Relationship

The political foundation for a German state that would eventually encompass a disparate group of independent kingdoms and principalities was not based on primordial ties of ethnicity, culture, or even language. While the common characteristic of language did eventually provide the material foundation for a common German identity, this attribute was not considered salient by the rulers until the reorganization of central Europe during the Napoleonic and post-Vienna periods created a special relationship among them. Like the discourse on the "Italian question," the external treatment of central Europe as part of a "German question" helped to nurture this idea.

When Napoleon's armies swept through central Europe, they confronted a complex set of overlapping institutions that resembled both medievalism and the ancien régime. Napoleon rationalized the hodgepodge of fiefdoms, ecclesiastical territories, and electorates that comprised the Holy Roman Empire by consolidating the territories into principalities and creating the Confederation of the Rhine. For the first time the German principalities achieved sovereign statehood independent of the Holy Roman Empire.[10]

After the defeat of France in 1814 the Congress of Vienna maintained most of Napoleon's reforms. Thirty-nine sovereign German states were loosely associated through the German Confederation. The confederation consisted of small Lutheran states in the south and Catholic provinces of Austria in the north. In the southwest there was a bloc of several relatively large kingdoms and principalities. The confederation was based on the concept of dualism, that is, joint management between Austria, which held the presidency, and Prussia, which assumed the vice presidency. Before 1848 neither Austria nor Prussia were interested in either altering the structure or in challenging the other. Austria made no effort to increase the powers of the presidency and Prussia accepted its secondary role.[11]

Like Napoleon, the great powers neither intended nor wished to create a German state. Rather, both saw administrative benefit in linking the German principalities and kingdoms together through a loose confederation under great power management. For the congress, this was vital to the concept of a strong independent European center.[12] However, as an unintended consequence, the organization of central Europe also created a special relationship among states that previously had little in common. In the first place, the confederation gave the hodgepodge of German states a unique collective identity. This was reinforced by the creation of institutional structures within the confederation that were exclusively "German" in membership. For the first time there was a concept of collective defense and security interdependence among historic rivals. Catholic and Protestant states became allies under the banner of the confederation.

Moreover, as in the case of Italy, the congress isolated the region from European politics by placing it exclusively within the sphere of the two German great powers. By treating the thirty-seven principalities and kingdoms as a political problem to be managed, the congress reinforced their unique relationship. The region later came to be known as the Third Germany. Finally, the congress had made Prussia more "German" by taking away its traditional Polish territories and allowing it to expand into the Rhineland. As a result, the Prussian kingdom's center of gravity shifted from Poland (its traditional political base) to the Germanic territories.[13]

The legacy of Vienna was therefore a concept of three Germanys: Hapsburg Germany, Hohenzollern Germany, and a Germany of small independent principalities. This would have an important impact on the future of central Europe.

1848 and the Changing Conceptions of Central Europe

The permissive condition that allowed for a redefinition of identities within central Europe was the undermining of existing authorities. Beginning with a liberal revolt in Baden in February 1848, uprisings spread to most of the other central European states. The fragility of the governments was evident by the speed at which the kings and princes capitulated to liberal demands; rebels gained power in almost every state, changing the complexion of the Federal Diet.[14] By March the revolution triumphed in Berlin (the capital of Prussia) and by October Vienna fell to the rebels.[15] The revolutions in Vienna and Hungary badly damaged the image of Austria as a German power by highlighting its multiethnic character and undermining its dynastic tradition. On the other hand, the Berlin revolution forced Prussia to grapple with its internal identity for the first time since 1701, when it became an independent state. The challenge to the Hohenzollern monarchy, which had been intricately identified with Prussia, raised the question of what Prussia was.

Out of this disorder and redefinition of authority, several alternative ideas for organizing central Europe emerged. There were essentially four proposed forms: a *Kleindeutsch* (Little Germany), a *Grossdeutsch* (Great Germany), a "triad" of Prussia, Austria, and a federated Germany comprised of the principalities, and a bipolar division of the region between Austria in the south and Prussia in the north. These forms were debated among German rulers, revolutionaries, and intellectuals throughout the 1848–1866 period, beginning with the Frankfort Parliament of 1848–1849. The Frankfort Parliament, also called the German Constituent National Assembly, was established in the midst of the German-wide revolutions by newly empowered liberal members of the various German diets. Its members were elected from all German states, including Prussia and Austria, for the purpose of developing a constitution for a united German state. The debate over the type of security arrangement that would replace the one imposed by the great powers at Vienna highlighted the disagreement over where conceptual boundaries should be drawn.

The Kleindeutsch solution foresaw a unified national state that would include all parts of the old German confederation except for Austria. This was based on the belief that the Austrian Empire was primarily non-German in composition and that since Austria was unwilling break up its empire it could not be part of a German national state. It was generally accepted that a Kleindeutsch state would be created by Prussia, the true heir to the German nation.[16] According to one German scholar, Prussia had a mission to create a united independent Germany under Hohenzollern leadership. "The time of powers, of dynastic issues is past; the principle of states, of citizenship in states, takes their place."[17] In this sense, Prussia (like Piedmont) was viewed by some as a positive referent society that embodied the transnational German identity.

The Kleindeutsch scenario saw the Prussian king as assuming the crown of Germany, although the early advocates of this solution also foresaw a national parliament and ministerial responsibility.[18] This approach was proposed by the president of the Frankfort Parliament, Heinrich von Gagern, and generally supported by the Protestant states from north and central Germany. Gagern argued against including non-German territories in the new state, saying the Parliament must

> recognize that Austria, for the time being, cannot enter the narrow federal state which the rest of Germany desires . . . because the majority of Austrians do not accept the conditions of entry into the narrower federal sense, namely the constitutional separation of the German provinces from the non-German ones.[19]

While 80 percent of Prussians were German, only eight million of the thirty-six million Austrians were Germanic; sixteen million were Slavs, five million were Hungarians, five were million Italians, and two million were Romanians.[20] A member of the Prussian Lower House of Parliament emphasized this point in a debate over the Austrian alliance in Germany: "If the Minister of the Interior . . . is regrettably going to repeat the phrase 'cooperation with Austria,' then I must reiterate: Austria is not German . . . to go hand in hand with Austria is to cooperate with twenty-eight million Slavs and others."[21]

Paul Pfizer, a Swabian minister from Baden, argued that a united Germany was not possible so long as two great powers were members of the German Confederation. He suggested that Austria must be excluded, since its far-flung interests in the Danube region and Italy would prevent it from fully identifying with the German nation.[22] A Kleindeutsch solution would destroy the system that the great powers had imposed on Europe by creating a national state that was independent from external forces.

A second alternative was the Grossdeutsch solution: a Germany of seventy million people including the territories of Prussia, Austria, and Bohemia but excluding the rest of the Hapsburg domains. In other words, it would be a state whose borders would coincide with those of the post-1815 German Confederation. This was supported primarily by the southern German states, all of which had Catholic majorities.[23] Even at the Frankfort Parliament, where most delegates sympathized with Prussia, there was great admiration for Austria's traditions and a strong desire to maintain links with the Hapsburgs.[24] Ex-Austrian revolutionary Julius Fröbel, for example, proposed a new German Empire with a central diet comprised of two houses. The house of princes would be led by a Prussian president and the emperorship would be hereditary in the Hapsburg dynasty.[25] This mirrored the organization of the German Confederation.

The Grossdeutsch approach was more complex—and thus less popular among the lesser German states—than the Kleindeutsch. While there was little doubt about the Germanic nature of Prussia—even among those states that distrusted her—it was unclear whether the Austrian Empire was a union of *two* states, one German, the other Magyar, or whether it was a single empire in which no nationality predominated.[26] This issue was crucial. If it was the former, then a Grossdeutsch state would be consistent with the national principle. Thus, the German and Bohemian territories of the empire could become part of the new state. On the other hand, if it was the latter, any entrance of Austria into Germany would automatically make it a multinational entity.

The three Germanys approach proposed the creation of a triad consisting of Prussia, Austria, and a federation of the German kingdoms and lesser German states. The Third Germany would be a federation rather than a unitary state, allowing each of the secondary powers to retain their independence but enabling them to act collectively as a coherent power. In a sense, it would be like the German Confederation without the domination of either Austria or Prussia. "Germany" would become a pluralistic security community. This concept of a triad was proposed at various times by the four German kingdoms: Baden, Württemberg, Bavaria, and Saxony. The idea of a separate identity for the secondary states could be traced to Napoleon's Confederation of the Rhine and to the common relationship these states had to the other great powers.

This concept of a "rump Germany" was further developed during the Frankfurt Parliament in 1848, when the initiative for German unity was shifted from the great powers to the secondary states. While Austria and Prussia were both Germanic in varying degrees, they were also members of the club of great powers, and in this sense were seen by many to have less in common with the other German states. Moreover, all the secondary states were at various times suspicious and fearful of Prussia and Austria. One version of the triad envisioned a third Germany that would be built under the leadership of Bavaria, as a counterpoise to Austria and Prussia.[27] This would have created a classic balance of power system in central Europe. Another version, offered by Badenese foreign minister Franz von Roggenbach, proposed a United States of Germany that would have excluded Austria but allowed Prussia representation. This would have given maximum power and independence to the states within the Third Germany. Von Roggenbach argued that

> the federal unity to be established should not be exclusive and unconditional, but that it should be one within which the independence

and sovereignty of the several existing federal states should continue undisturbed over the whole area of domestic legislation and administration.[28]

Freidrich von Buest from Saxony suggested creating a federal diet that would meet in the north under a Prussian presidency and in the south under an Austrian one. There would also be a parliament of delegates from the German states that would compose the institutions of a united Germany. Opposing a German federal state, Buest argued that a "league of states, to which Germany owes its finest flowering of her cultural life" is the best solution.[29] What each of these proposals had in common was a desire to create a separate identity for the secondary German states, avoiding domination by either great power but also falling short of creating a German state. It would be a clear rejection of pan-Germanism, and parochial identities would trump transnational ones. The most ambitious effort to put this idea into practice was the creation of the Four Kings Alliance by Saxony, Hanover, Württemberg, and Bavaria in 1850, an attempt that ultimately failed.

The Third Germany approach was rejected for reasons both internal and external to the German states. Externally, it would have meant excluding two historic German great powers, Prussia and Austria. This would have been difficult unless it was accompanied by successful revolution in either Prussia and Austria, since both powers would have likely objected to the creation of a new great power in central Europe. For Austria, it would have meant severing its ties with the German states; for Prussia, it would call into question its very existence as a German state. While revolutions were initially successful in these countries, they were soon suppressed. Internally, there was little unity among the princes and the politically active population. For example, the Frankfurt Parliament was born out of revolution and thus did not represent the princes but rather those actors recently empowered by the revolutions. So long as the liberals and radicals were in control of the German diets, the deputies to the parliament could speak for their states. However, once the revolutions were defeated, the Frankfurt Parliament became irrelevant.

At the same time, none of the four kingdoms seriously tried to lead a German revolution or challenge Austria or Prussia when the great powers were vulnerable. As a result, there was no positive referent society around which the Third Germany could coalesce.

Support within the German Confederation vacillated between these alternatives, and even within Prussia and Austria opinion was divided. While it might seem obvious that Prussia would support Kleindeutsch and Austria Grossdeutsch, this was not obvious during the 1848–1866 period. Here is a clear case in which interests followed the definition of the situation. For example, if it was Prussia's natural interest to dominate central Europe, why didn't it attempt to unify Germany under its leadership in 1849 rather than 1866? The distribution of power clearly favored Prussia far more in 1848–1849 than in 1866–1870.[30] Austria was occupied with internal revolts and military conflicts in Hungary and Italy, and Vienna itself was undergoing widespread unrest. Russia was preoccupied with the revolts in Poland, the Danube, and Hungary. Internally, France was in disarray resulting from its own revolution. Not only did the international situation favor a Prussian-led Germany, but Prussia's internal position would have been greatly improved by such a move; domestically, the monarchy was under strong pressure to pursue liberal and national policies, including the unification of Germany.

The Prussians did not view the situation within this framework, however. King Frederick William IV revered what he saw as the centuries-old tradition of the Holy Roman Empire. The idea of a new Germany that would sweep away the Holy Roman heritage, the rights of the princes, and their royal institutions was totally alien to him.[31] He did not favor a Little German approach, arguing that "Germany without the Tyrol, Trieste and the Archduchy (Austria) would be worse than a nose without a face."[32] Thus, while Prussia may have benefited geopolitically from a Kleindeutsch state, this was not its preferred outcome until the 1864–1866 period. Up to that point, Prussia remained faithful to the alliance of central European great powers.

This point was made most blatantly when Prussian king Frederick William rejected the crown of Germany that was offered to him by the Frankfurt Parliament in 1849. His reasons for the rejection were twofold, both related to his transnational identities as a European monarch and leader of a European great power. First, he would not accept a "crown from the gutter" (the people), insisting that he could only accept such an offer if it came from the legitimate German princes.[33] Moreover, he did not want to extinguish Prussia's identity, saying, "The colors black, red, and gold (the flag of the German nation) shall not supplant my cockade, the honored colors of black and white (the symbol of the House of Hohenzollern)."[34] Second, his image of a German Reich was not based on Prussian aggrandizement, but on a Christian Germany ruled by the House of Hapsburg with himself as second in command in charge of the federal army.[35] He was thus looking toward an imperial central European alliance between Little Germany and the whole of the Hapsburg domains.

From the Austrian perspective there was no obvious state interest apart from the interests of the dominant political actors within the empire. The 1815–1848 period had been characterized by a close transnational political alliance among the German aristocracies that cut across political boundaries.[36] Austria's conservative aristocracy had a deep admiration for Prussia and hoped for a renewal of the old class coalition with the Prussian aristocracy as late as 1860.[37] Class solidarity, not state power, was their primary focus.

Austria's unwillingness to give up its multinational empire ultimately made the Grossdeutsch approach impossible. This was not lost on the German states, for while Prussia was considered a decidedly *German* power, Austria was viewed more as a *European* one.[38] Although this was an advantage under the Vienna system, after 1848 it became a liability. However, for Austria, the conflict was between the national principle and the imperial ideal, and there was never any question as to which the Austrian monarch would choose, even if it meant sacrificing Austria's position in central Europe. In fact, Emperor Francis Joseph enacted policies that he knew would likely weaken his influence with the German principalities in the interest of facilitating greater internal coherence within the empire. In March 1849 he promulgated a new constitution that subjected all parts of the Austrian Empire to control from Vienna. This created a single united empire, and that automatically precluded an Austrian-led German state, since none of the proposals envisioned including the Hungarian lands in the German nation.[39]

This consolidation of the Hapsburg empire led to the weakening of ties between the Austrian state and the German nation.[40] Faced with a choice between remaining a central European multinational empire and expanding into a new central European nation-state, Austria opted for its parochial loyalties. While Prussia eventually adopted a Little German policy, the Hapsburgs never showed a willingness to trade their Hungarian territories for rule over central Europe. This made it impossible for Austria to become a positive reference group embodying the German ideal.

In fact, like Prussia, Austria passed over several opportunities to create a German state with Vienna as its head. Between 1815 and the 1860s Austria had the sympathy of many of the smaller German states, particularly those in the Catholic south.[41] Yet while the Hapsburgs made several more bids for German *leadership* (the final one being the Congress of German Princes in 1863), unlike Prussia they never tried to organize an Austrian-led German state. Thus, even up until its dissolution, the Austrian empire chose to maintain its Hapsburg heritage. This, rather than an abstract notion of raison état, can explain its behavior during the 1849–1866 period.

The Prussian Dilemma

Prussia's evolution from an electorate within the Holy Roman Empire to an independent modern state was facilitated by the development of its bureaucratic structure, which flourished under both ministerial and absolute kings. With the growth of a strong administrative apparatus in the eighteenth century the state came to be regarded as something apart from the monarch.[42] The development of the state as a political force independent of the monarchy was precipitated by the rise of the Junkers. The Junkers were an aristocratic ruling class that became active in government, and, over time, they came to dominate the state bureaucracy. Frederick the Great had brought crown and state together by forging a close alliance between the monarchy and the Junker nobility, announcing, "I am the first servant of the state."[43] From this political arrangement three political forces developed within Prussia: the Hohenzollern dynasty, the bureaucratic state, and the German cultural nation.[44]

During the 1848 revolutions the spread of liberal ideas and the rise of the middle class challenged both the dominance of the Junker nobility (and thereby the state itself) and the idea of dynastic lineage as a justification for rule.[45] The speed at which the king and military capitulated to the rebellion in Berlin undermined the image of the state as all powerful. Coupled with the European-wide rebellion against the Vienna system, the ruling classes of the German states lost their authority. These multiple challenges greatly weakened the entire concept of great power security management and monarchic solidarity in central Europe. Yet, while the authority of the monarchy was challenged, the liberals never succeeded in making Prussia into a constitutional state, and public opinion remained divided.[46] As a result, the country emerged from the 1848 period at a political stalemate.

The first casualty was the alliance between the Prussian state and the Hohenzollern monarchy. The leaders of both institutions were uncertain about where their loyalties would ultimately lie. As long as the Prussian state, the Hohenzollern crown, and the Junker class were united (as it had been during the eighteenth and early nineteenth centuries) Prussia's position as a European dynastic state was stable. While the French revolution and the Napoleonic wars challenged the legitimacy of both the dynasty and the state, the Vienna system created a new role for Prussia as a central European great power. The German revolutions and the Frankfurt Parliament brought the questions of German nationality and parliamentary government to the forefront. Both these forces challenged Prussia's identity as a German, dynastic Junker and bureaucratic state. This led to a division among the dominant institutions of Prussian society as to what Prussia was and what its role should be in central Europe.

Given the intensity of these domestic conflicts and the competing identities, it is difficult to identify a "Prussian interest" during the 1849–1966 period. Rather, there were competing interests among groups promoting different visions of Prussia's future. Security considerations would follow the resolution of this dilemma. Consequently, in order to understand Prussia's role in the creation of a German national state, one must take into account how different identities, both parochial and transnational, led to different conceptions of interest.

Prussia's internal division began during the Berlin revolution. In May of 1848 the king agreed to establish a representative Prussian National Assembly. The assembly immediately began to discuss the creation of a constitutional state, though not necessarily a national one.[47] As in the case of Italy, the main focus was not national unity but rather constitutionalism and representative government. In reaction to this development, the Junkers organized their own assembly, popularly dubbed the "Junker Parliament." These processes occurred simultaneously with the opening of the transnational (that is, pan-Germanic) Frankfurt Parliament.

By the fall, however, the army regained control of Berlin and closed the assembly. At the same time, the king agreed to adopt a moderately liberal constitution modeled after the Belgian charter of 1830.[48] While the Prussian army and conservative ministers wanted to defeat the nationalist movement and assert Prussian influence in Germany, Frederick William was neither a Prussian patriot nor a Junker king. Prussia's bureaucracy had to reconcile its position with the king's new romantic vision of Germany.[49] Thus developed the first serious division between the state and the crown.

Further complicating the domestic situation was the recovery of Austria after the defeat of the revolutions in Vienna, Hungary, and its Slavic territories. Emperor Frederick William had tried to reassert Austrian leadership by creating an "Erfurt Union" of the German kingdoms and secondary states. He was temporarily successful, bringing twenty-four German states into the union by early 1850.[50] Austria's success resulted in Prussia's isolation and ultimately its humiliation at Olmütz, ending any possibility of a new cooperative relationship between the central European powers.[51] This humiliation further undermined the prestige and power of the Prussian state, particularly the bureaucracy and army. The relegitimation of Prussia was now a necessity.

The Hohenzollern monarchy hoped to rebuild its dynastic authority in Prussia. During the 1815–1848 period Prussia's dual role as a European great power and legitimate dynastic house allowed for a fusion of parochial and transnational loyalties. It could continue to promote its dynastic interests within the context of Prussian state power, which was supported by its participation in the European concert and Holy Alliance. However, with the breakdown in solidarity among European monarchies—especially the split between the two German great powers—Prussian power and dynastic interests were no longer necessarily the same. In particular, the definitions of Germany and the means toward creating a German state diverged.

King Frederick William had been willing to subordinate Prussian ambitions to Austrian supremacy for the benefit of German unity, at least until the early 1850s.[52] Both he and his brother William were legitimists, believing in the rights of monarchs over the ambitions of states. When the king became incapacitated in 1858 and William assumed the throne, the crown declared its commitment to kingship through divine right.[53] Moreover, upon his accession, William expressed his hope for a "moral conquest" of Germany, arguing that "in Germany Prussia must make moral conquests by wise legislation of its own, by elevating all moral elements, and by adopting elements of unification. . . . The world must know that Prussia is ready everywhere to protect right."[54]

As a Hohenzollern, William wanted to absorb some of the smaller German states into Prussia by giving the princes a privileged place in governmental assemblies and by having them serve in the Hohenzollern army and bureaucracy. The crown valued its ties to the Hapsburgs and their shared history within the Holy Roman Empire.[55] This, however, soon brought the Hohenzollern monarchy into conflict with both the statist Bismarck and with the German nationalists inside Prussia.

During the 1850s conservative monarchists were more interested in maintaining monarchical government than in guaranteeing territorial sovereignty.[56] While the crown sought German unity through moral conquest, however, the Prussian state, as represented by the Junker-dominated bureaucracy and army, was primarily interested in increasing Prussian power. As a class, the Junkers were opposed to a German Empire; they considered themselves Prussians, not Germans, and felt a loyalty to their own state.[57] Their class interests were more important than any national feeling that could develop, and thus to some degree their fortunes were tied to the ex-istence of an independent Prussia, historically the guarantor of these interests.

Bismarck, a Junker who came to represent the Prussian state after his appointment as president-minister in 1862, was particularly opposed to hav-ing Prussia submerged into a German national state.[58] The Junkers clearly favored parochialism over transnationalism. As Bismarck told Italian General Govone, "I am much less a German than a Prussian";[59] he was initially opposed to a united Germany, even under Prussian leadership. "We are satisfied with the name Prussia," he stated, "and are proud of the name Prussia. . . . Prussian we are and Prussian we wish to remain."[60] Prussian patriotism, not pan-German nationalism, was his focus of loyalty. The state bureaucracy identified most with the legacy of Frederick the Great, who had built Prussia into a great power through a policy of conquest. The Prus-sian ministers and state officials were particularly incensed over the humil-iation suffered at Olmütz. To the extent that Austria had begun to treat Prussia as an object rather than as a partner, Prussian state officials no longer saw any bonds between them as German great powers. Austria became a negative reference other.

This conflict brought Bismarck and the other conservative ministers into conflict with King William. In the face of widespread social unrest in the mid-nineteenth century, the survival of the monarchy required more than an assertion of state power vis-à-vis other states. It demanded domestic sup-port and legitimation from a restless population. Thus, when Bismarck made his well-known statement, "The great questions of the day will not be de-cided by speeches and resolutions of majorities . . . but by iron and blood,"[61] King William was so appalled that he planned to immediately dismiss Bis-marck from the ministry.[62] While he was later talked out of making this move by his advisers, it is a good indication of the tension that existed be-tween crown and state.

The third political force to enter Prussian society after 1848 was trans-nationalism. The 1848 revolutions not only legitimized the idea of a pan-German *nationalism*, it also empowered the German *nationalists*. Before the German (and European) revolutions the population had no independent political existence apart from either state or monarch. This is why the Con-gress of Vienna could so easily redraw state boundaries without considering the populations that lived within them. After 1848, however, virtually all German princes were forced to grant constitutions to their people, thereby explicitly recognizing their political status. The people (at least the aristocracy) became citizens rather than subjects. The constitutional institutions remained even after absolutism was revived in Prussia and Austria in the early 1850s. Thus, the interests of the politically active segments of the population became an important political force.

The nationalists' loyalties were directed not to the monarch or the state but to the German nation, which cut across state borders. This was well articulated by the members of Prussia's German Progressive Party:

> The existence and greatness of Prussia depends upon a firm unification of Germany. . . .
>
> We work for no one dynasty in Germany, neither for the Hohenzollern nor for the Hapsburg, when we wish to establish German unity. We work for ourselves, the German people. . . .
>
> This majority recognizes no other than German interests, and that if in some way the so-called Prussian interests should conflict with the German interests, we prefer the German interests.[63]

While the nationalist and liberal movements receded after the restoration of state and monarchic authority in 1850, they regained their strength in 1859, after the Italian war of liberation sparked national enthusiasm for liberation in Germany. The political expression of this sentiment was manifested through the formation of the Nationalverein (National Society), modeled after the organization that helped facilitate Italian integration.

Legitimation and the Prussian Constitutional Crisis

The tensions described above led to the crises of 1860–1864. For the next four years Prussia was locked in an internal conflict over different types of reform: constitutional, tax, military, social, political, and parliamentary. Prussia could neither play a major role in international affairs nor assert itself as a state until its internal political struggle between liberals and conservatives, parliament and crown was resolved.[64] In the 1861 elections the Progressive Party swept the Lower House of the Lantag (Prussian Parliament), prompting the king to dissolve the parliament and call for new elections. The new election brought in an even larger liberal majority.

The conflict between crown and parliament culminated in the battle over military reform. Both the army (the state) and the king (the monarchy) wanted to change the length of service and method of financing for the Prussia army. While the issue may have been divisive on its own merits, it raised a more fundamental question, "Who rules Prussia?" or, more specifically, "Who *is* Prussia?" King William argued that those opposing military reform were "seeking to limit the highest attribute of royalty, the war command."[65] Thus the king was defending the rule of the Hohenzollern monarchy.

At the same time, the army and bureaucracy were defending the power of the state against encroachments from civil society, represented by the parliament. After the Lantag voted down the budget, the Prussian government was paralyzed. Despondent over his inability to run the government, King William considered resigning. On the verge of abdication, he appointed Bismarck as minister-president, "who assumed the role of a feudal vassal come to learn his lord's will."[66] Thus, Bismarck was not brought into the Prussian government either to unify Germany or to increase Prussian power but rather to resolve the constitutional crisis.

Transnational Identity as a Unifying Force

The crisis forced the political actors within Prussia to address the questions of Prussia's identity and its role in the European system. Unlike Austria, which was comfortable with its position as a multinational empire under the Hapsburg monarchy, Prussia was a divided society. Its behavior from 1863–1871—the period of integration—reflects this division. At this point, questions of domestic politics and transnational identities intersected. The revival of "the German question" occurred over the dispensation of the duchies of Schleswig and Holstein.

Under the Vienna treaties of 1815 Schleswig and Holstein were tied to the Danish monarchy through a personal union. Holstein, however, was Germanic and had been part of the Holy Roman Empire; in 1815 it joined the German Confederation. Schleswig had been a Danish province since the ninth century; however, it had a majority Germanic population. Despite the common monarch, the duchies were covered by royal succession laws that were different from those of Denmark.

This had led to a crisis in 1848, when Frederick VII assumed the throne of Denmark. One of his first acts was to sign a document declaring the Danish monarchy to be indivisible through a complete territorial and constitutional union between Denmark and Schleswig and the subjection of both duchies to the Danish crown law.[67] This led to a revolt in the duchies, and a resurgence in national feeling within Germany.[68] Under strong pressure from nationalists throughout the German principalities, Prussia invaded and occupied the duchies. The war was ended in part through pressure from the great powers but also because King Frederick William was disturbed that he had supported a revolt against a legitimate monarch.[69]

This issue once again emerged in 1863, while Prussia was in the middle of its constitutional crisis. The Danish parliament passed a new constitution that incorporated Schleswig into the Danish kingdom, effectively separating the two duchies. This was not only a violation of the London Treaty of 1852, which ended the first war, but it was perceived by the German public to be an attack on German nationality. Once again, this excited nationalist sentiment within the German states. For the first time, the German states proposed building an alliance based solely on their transnational ties. National parliaments throughout the German Confederation called for a war of liberation to install Frederick of Augustenberg as duke of Schleswig-Holstein. The Prussian parliament voiced its support for war in national terms: "The honor and the interests of Germany require that the German states as a whole should recognize the Hereditary Prince Frederick as Duke of Schleswig-Holstein and should render him effective assistance in the assertion of his rights.[70] With the support of the German Confederation the German armies forced the Danish out of the duchies; in the peace agreement that ended the war, Denmark ceded them to Prussia and Austria jointly.

This was the first time that all the German states fought together as Germans. The continued interest of the German and Danish people in Schleswig-Holstein from 1846–1866 was due not to its strategic importance but to the fierce clash between German and Danish nationalism in the area between the Eider and Kongea rivers.[71] At the same time, the issue of what to do with the duchies raised broader questions concerning the relationships between Austria, Prussia, and the German states. German nationalists favored the installation of the German prince of Augustenberg as head of an independent German duchy. This would have placed the Germanic peoples of the duchies under a German monarch.

Monarchic solidarity favored the prince on legitimist grounds, but dynastic interests would not be served by the creation of yet another small independent German state. The Prussian state interest encouraged annexation to Prussia. Austria's interest as an empire was to include the duchies in the German confederation under the duelist administration of the two German great powers. Thus, Schleswig-Holstein was a microcosm for the German question in general. This is why the conflicts that erupted over these minor duchies inevitably led to conflict over the future of Germany.

The conflict over the duchies represented the competing understandings of what constituted Germany. The addition of a newly independent German principality to the existing German confederation would represent a victory for the Third Germany approach. That is, the emphasis would have been placed on the duchies' particularlism and their loose affiliation with other German states. Annexation to Prussia would have lent support to the idea of a kleindeutsch Germany, since the emphasis would have been on the duchies' German nationality rather than on their particularlist affiliations with the house of Augustenberg. With annexation to Prussia, its supremacy as a German state would have been strengthened. The incorporation of the new duchies into the duelist German confederation would have maintained the unity of a grossdeutsch Germany without creating a unified state. It would have emphasized a Germany that included Austria without requiring Austria to give up its non-German lands.

Thus Austria regarded the German Confederation from the perspective of its role as a central European empire. From this standpoint German unity was never a serious consideration. The Austrian Germans identified with the Hapsburg dynasty more than with their German brethren in the principalities. Their loyalty was to their great empire and they did not want to see that empire destroyed in the name of German nationalism.[72] Moreover, as Austria began to shift the focus of its empire from Vienna to Budapest, it became less tied to the interests of the German principalities. Austria's priority of maintaining its empire was be made clear in 1866; in the midst of its war against Prussia over the future of Germany, Austria sent 130,000 soldiers to fight Italy over control of Venice at a time when they were badly needed at the Prussian front.[73]

Prussia, on the other hand, was divided over its role in Germany, and, moreover, it was still gripped in an internal crisis over its identity as a state. These differences, both domestic and international, were played out over the Schleswig-Holstein question and the war against Austria. While Bismarck favored annexation of the duchies to Prussia, both the king and the crown prince were horrified at this suggested violation of the legitimist principle.[74] Nationalist opinion rested squarely with the duke of Augustenberg as the legitimate German ruler. Bismarck's interests were tied to those of the Prussian state. Aside from territorial considerations, he was interested in the possibility of Prussia gaining a naval harbor, which would enhance the prestige and power of the state.[75] Moreover, he wished to exclude Austria from German affairs, partly to repay them for the humiliation at Omültz. He thus sought to provoke a war with Austria to settle the German question once and for all.[76]

The crown, on the other hand, saw the issue as a German rather than a Prussian one and favored recognizing Prince Frederick of Augustenberg as

the legitimate ruler.[77] King William argued that Prussia had no moral claim
to the duchies.[78] While Bismarck saw Prussian concerns as the priority, the
crown held German and monarchic interests to be dominant. When Bismarck argued that Prussia's goal should be to force Denmark to recognize
the Treaty of London (granting governing rights to Denmark), King William
exclaimed to him, "Aren't you a German at all?"[79] Bismarck, of course, was
a German, but he was also a Prussian, and as a representative of the Prussian
state this was his priority.

Almost until the war with Austria began, the crown favored maintaining
Prussia's alliance with Austria. As late as 1865, for example, King William
spoke of the German great power alliance's "firm and enduring foundation
in My German patriotism and that of My ally."[80] He reflected, "What mis-
fortune we should create and what offense we should give to the world if
we two, the son of Frederick William III and the grandson of the Emperor
Francis, were to turn from being friends and allies into enemies?"[81] This
view was shared by legitimist minister Ludwig von Gerlack who argued that

> the dualism is the vital basis, the real foundation, of the German Con-
> stitution. Germany ceases to the Germany without Prussia or without
> Austria. Prussia's honor and power are therefore the pride of Germany
> and Austria's honor and power are the pride of Prussia. To injure
> Prussia is to injure Austria, and to injure Austria is to injure Prussia.[82]

When Bismarck argued for war during a council of ministers meeting in
February of 1866, the crown prince argued that such an act would be "frat-
ricide and a crime against German nationality."[83] He said he would attend
no more meetings until Bismarck resigned.

The German nationalists both within and outside Prussia favored integration at almost any cost. While many of the German princes supported
Austria before and during the war of 1866, the interests of their parliaments
and political organizations coincided with those of Prussia.[84] Within the
German states public and elite opinion was divided over their relationship
with Prussia. While many of the kings of the larger states were wary of
Prussian power, liberals in the parliaments gave priority to German
integration.[85]

A Common Experience: Standing Together as Germans

The war of 1866 came about despite the reservations of the Prussian
crown, partly because of Bismarck's provocations but also because Austria

had tried to use the German Confederation as a tool to isolate and humiliate Prussia.[86] Contemporaries, both pro- and anti-Prussian, referred to this war as the German Revolution or the German Civil War rather than as a hegemonic war between two great powers.[87] The Prussian victory ended Austria's role in Germany and led to the construction of the first amalgamated security community in central Europe: the North German Confederation under Prussian leadership. This security community was created as an all-German association based on a unique relationship among its members.

Prussia's policy after the war reflected the tension between its parochial and transnational identities. Bismarck wanted to annex Hanover, Hesse-Kassel, and Nassau to Prussia in order to undo the forced separation of the eastern and western half of Prussia. This separation had been created by the Congress of Vienna when Prussia was induced to trade its Polish territories for lands on the Rhineland. It had since become a state objective to extend its influence over the territories separating the old mark of Brandenberg from the Rhineland.[88]

King William, on the other hand, was strongly opposed to the dethronement of legitimate princely dynasties as being incompatible with monarchical principles.[89] This view was shared by the feudalist Conservative Party (to which Bismarck was nominally a member). William, however, finally agreed to the annexations not only for reasons of Prussian aggrandizement but in fact to punish the princes who had treasonously taken up arms against him.[90]

The Prussian victory and the creation of a security community increased transnational pressure on the central European leaders. The victory sparked an impassioned outburst of national feeling throughout Germany, even within states that had supported Austria.[91] Prussia's status was elevated as the symbol of pan-German unity. In the three months following the Prussian victory over Austria, Bismarck accepted the necessity of placing German interests alongside Prussian ambitions.[92] While he had strongly opposed German integration throughout the 1848–1866 period, after the war he realized that only German nationalism could legitimize authority within the North German Confederation and, more specifically, within Prussia. The constitutional conflict and the rebellions within the principalities had demonstrated that the population identified more with their German heritage than with either the Hohenzollern dynasty or the Prussian state.

Upon becoming the federal chancellor of the newly formed North German Federation, Bismarck remarked that it was his duty to "develop the power of Germany and not that of a greater Prussia."[93] Whether Bismarck the individual was simply responding to political pressure rather than expressing changing sentiments is irrelevant. In his role as executive of an amalgamated security community he had to redefine Prussia's interest in transnational (that is, pan-Germanic) terms. Thus, while he had not given up his policy of realpolitik, his interests were no longer Prussian, but German. This change was not only in name but would have an effect on the course of history.

During the late 1860s the economic and social habits of the newly annexed western territories began to transform the character of the old Prussian state. With the integration of different Germanic cultures they began to take on a new "German," rather than a traditional "Prussian" character. The constitution of the North German Confederation was a synthesis between Hohenzollern monarchism, Prussian statism, and German nationalism. The will of the nation was satisfied through the creation of a common German citizenship for all independent states. The franchise for the Parliament was universal (male) suffrage and it recognized both the German people and the princes. The interests of the states were protected through the Bundestrat, the executive body comprised of representatives from state governments. The king of Prussia maintained his dynastic tie by assuming the leadership of the Reich.

Thus, it would be simplistic to view the creation of the confederation as simply a Prussianization of the north.[94] The sharp divisions within Prussia make it clear that power considerations were only one element in determining the type of security arrangements they would construct. Moreover, the integration of the new provinces into Prussia progressed rapidly after 1866 because the national sentiments of the population became stronger than their local loyalties.[95] The North German Confederation began to change the outlook of the smaller and medium-size German states; by participating in the security community, their leaders began to think and act like Germans. Reflecting and assisting this transformation was the replacement of the Prussian flag with a new German banner.

While the North German Confederation continued to develop a uniquely German identity, the question of the south German kingdoms remained. By 1866 Bismarck realized that the construction of a pan-German state required that the south be won over, not conquered. Unity depended on the voluntary cooperation of the princely dynasties.[96] He thus recognized that German unity would have no permanence in the absence of a transnational German identity among the major political forces in central Europe. Moreover, he understood that the biggest impediment to the creation of a united German state was the particularism of the princely dynasties in both the north and south.

Unlike a dynastic state, a national state depends upon the will of the nation for its legitimation. Understanding this, Bismarck promoted the idea of a national representative parliament as a key part of the central government. This was necessary not only for establishing a unifying force among the divergent states but also as a counterbalance to "the diverging tendencies of dynastic special policies."[97] To this end, Bismarck concluded alliance agreements with the four south German kingdoms.

In the end, however, it took one more war—this one against France—to truly unify Germany. As Otto Pflanze perceptively argues, "the cult of the nation requires devils as well as gods. If Bismarck was the [George] Washington of the German revolution, [Louis] Napoleon was its [King] George III."[98] Prussia became a positive reference group in sharp distinction from a negative one, France. Thus, the German Empire was the outcome of a war in which all the German states fought together as a transnational community against a common enemy. While the war began over an obscure dynastic issue, the shared battles, shared victories, and occasional losses turned it into a transnational crusade.[99] The psychological bond established between the German states during the war diminished the particularistic sentiments, dynastic loyalties, and local customs that had previously divided them.

It had been generally accepted within the principalities that the conflict with France was truly a German, not a Prussian, quarrel,[100] this despite the fact that France declared war on Prussia alone and not against the south German states. However, through its bellicose rhetoric, France had turned a dynastic issue into a German national one.[101] This helped lead to a shift in public and elite sentiment from parochialism to transnationalism, particularly within the south German states. Their interests were defined in German rather than parochial terms. Whether or not Bismarck conspired to provoke the war remains a historical controversy.[102] What is important for our purposes is the role of this common experience in strengthening the states' transnational identities.

The final stage in the integration of Germany required all the parties to give up at least some of their particularist loyalties. After the war of 1870 the southern kingdoms entered into agreements with the North German Confederation to create a single unified German state. The Prussian state was transformed through the resurrection of the title of Kaiser and the concept of the Reich, both of which had historical roots in the German nation. King Louis of Bavaria, for example, bid King William to "re-establish the

German *Reich* and the German imperial dignity."[103] The newly established German constitution decreed one common nationality and guaranteed that "every person belonging to any one of the confederated states should be treated in every other of those states as a born native with equal rights."[104] Thus, it was not a process of Prussification but one rather of Germanification that united the central European states.

The process that led to the integration of Germany demonstrates how the evolution of transnational identities can help to diminish the conceptual boundaries that separate societies. The creation of Germany became *possible* when the revolutions of 1848 undermined domestic authority and changed the balance of power in central Europe. It became *likely*, however, when the rulers and populations of Prussia and the German principalities placed their *transnational* identities as Germans ahead of their own *particularistic* identities. While these revolutions undermined the legitimacy of the monarchies and the Vienna system in general, no political group emerged dominant, and thus domestic conflicts paralyzed much of Prussia and the German states. Identification with the German nation, strengthened through wars against Denmark and France, proved to be the single force that could unite the rulers and active populations across class and ideological lines.

These conflicts ultimately led to the creation of an amalgamated security community in the north and ultimately to full political integration. Within Austria the Hapsburg rulers and the Magyar (Hungarian) nationalists ultimately chose to defend the position as a multiethnic empire, effectively ending any possibility of a grossdeutsch solution. In Prussia transnationalism helped to harmonize what had become competing institutions within the state: the Hohenzollern crown, the Prussian bureaucracy, the Junker aristocracy, and the German constitutionalists. This enabled Prussia to emerge as a positive reference group for the smaller German principalities embodying the German ideal. While history tends to focus on Bismarck's statist policies as the force that brought about German integration, this chapter has demonstrated that the raison of Prussia depended upon the type of état it would become. Despite different conceptions of Prussian and German identities, Bismarck and the liberal nationalists ultimately agreed on their fundamental understanding of Germany; they each needed the other.

The conflict between Austria and Prussia cannot be reduced to a hegemonic clash between two great powers seeking to increase their relative power. While it *was* a power struggle, the fundamental conflict was as much over what each state was and would become than it was one over control of central Europe. These differences cannot be accounted for by a simple notion of raison d'état. I have argued that the key tension in the integration process was between parochialism and transnationalism. This helped to define state interests. From late 1848 Austria had several opportunities to build a unified German state under its leadership, particularly when Prussia was weak. Yet this would have meant abandoning its Hapsburg Empire legacy, something few Austrians were willing to do. Austria's unwillingness to undergo the changes necessary to evolve from a multinational empire to a national state made it ultimately impossible for it to lead the German nation. Prussia, on the other hand, was strengthened by its transnational ties, and it was ultimately German nationalism that enabled the Prussian state to recover from its internal turmoil. The price was the cession of sovereignty to create a new political community.

Part 3

Conclusion

6 *Transnational Community in an Anarchic World*

Living in an anarchic world, one hesitates to think in terms of transnational community. Every generation since the birth of the nation-state system has had to cope with various forms of interstate conflict, rivalry, and mutual suspicion. Without external guarantees, trust is not easy to establish even with the best of intentions. As Woody Allen once observed, the lion will lie down with the lamb, but the lamb will not get much sleep that night. Yet, as the previous chapters have demonstrated, under certain conditions political actors can and have chosen to pursue cohesive security arrangements rather than competitive rivalries.

Much of European history has been characterized by dynastic rivalry, hegemonic conflict, shifting balances, and partitions of sovereign states. Yet, as the empirical chapters have demonstrated, there was a fundamental change in European interstate relations in the nineteenth century. Using the standards of measurement and evidence outlined in chapter 1, the cases suggest that states did indeed develop positive transnational identities after 1815 and 1848. Although rivalry and suspicion continued on one level, there was also strong evidence of ideological solidarity, group cohesion, and a sense of a common good, at least among a group of state elites.

Despite the obstacles posed by a competitive international environment, states do build special relationships with other states that go beyond simple expediency. This book has tried to theorize about how and why these relationships develop. It found that the key variable that explains the construction of cohesive security arrangements is transnational identity. Transnational identities can transform egoistic conceptions of sovereignty into perceptions of commonality by facilitating the notion of a common good. To the extent that states are conscious of themselves as constituting a social group, they develop a communality of interests. When such a consciousness is achieved and the idea of a common good accepted, the foundation for a transnational political community is created. The type of identity determines the type of community.

In this concluding chapter I will flesh out the theoretical implications of this study and examine how they can help us to sort out the possibilities for the post–cold war order. In the first section I will revisit the hypotheses outlined in chapter 2 in light of the empirical evidence. I will then discuss how this study contributes to the body of international relations theory and offer possibilities for future research. Finally, I will examine the future of security arrangements after the cold war.

Evaluating the Evidence

Kenneth Waltz argues that structural theories gain plausibility if similarities of behavior are observed across realms that are different in substance but similar in structure.[1] It follows, then, that a structural theory will *lose* plausibility if *differences* of behavior are observed across realms that are similar in structure. If this is so, then the security arrangements that emerged in the periods following the Napoleonic wars and the revolutions of 1848 suggest that the distribution of capabilities as an explanatory variable is at best indeterminate. These arrangements were not consistent with multipolar systems during other periods of European history, nor was the behavior of the actors consistent with what structural theories would predict given the conditions at the time.

The cases of the concert and the Holy Alliance support the theses that state actors can indeed share transnational identities with other actors and that this can lead to the creation of cohesive security arrangements. Using the standards of evidence articulated in chapter 1, the empirical chapters found the following: first, there were consistent patterns in the way the political leaders of the great powers and eastern monarchies described themselves and their interaction partners. Specifically, there was a clear sense that they constituted unique communities of great powers and monarchs and that this did not extend to other states. In spite of ongoing tension, they approached the major issues dealing with European reconstruction, revolution, and security from discernible European, great power, and monarchic perspectives. There was also a clear concept of a common good: an aristocratic Europe of monarchies in which security was collectively managed by a small group of mutually acknowledged great powers.

If group cohesion (as opposed to simple cooperation) is evidence of a moderate, positive transnational identity, the Concert of Europe represents the institutionalization of a great power community. Based on a behavioral analysis, I found that the actions of the state leaders were inconsistent with what one should have expected given the structural conditions in the postwar era, absent a common identity. While internal conflict emerged during the concert period, three important indicators of group cohesion are indisputable: the number of potential crises the great powers collectively diffused, the willingness of the powers not to exploit these crises for their own gain, and the steadfast commitment not to go outside the great power circle to solicit allies, even when such action could have been advantageous.

Beginning with the dispute over Poland and Saxony at the Congress of Vienna, the great powers faced many potentially divisive challenges: the reintegration of France into the European community barely three years after the final defeat of Napoleon, conflicts over the eastern question, the independence of Greece and Belgium, rebellion in Spain and within the German and Italian states, the growing ideological division between the conservative monarchies of the east and the parliamentary governments of the west, and, ultimately, the revolutions of 1848. In a balance of power system any one of these crises could have easily escalated into war or at least would likely have led to the emergence of competing power blocs. Instead, all these crises were settled within the club of great powers, specifically within the context of congress diplomacy. Despite ongoing disagreements over how the congress system should operate, none of the great powers pursued unilateral action once an issue was declared to be European in nature.

To gain a perspective on this situation, compare the aftermath of the Congress of Vienna to that of the Yalta conference following World War II. In both cases the major powers attempted to create security systems based on great power management and spheres of responsibility (Roosevelt's four policemen), yet both also had the potential to break up into two opposing blocs.[2] After the Napoleonic wars Britain and Russia each had the capabilities to dominate the continent, yet instead of competing for European hegemony they pooled their resources to jointly manage security affairs.

The crises faced by the great powers from 1815 through 1822 were potentially just as great as those between the East and the West in the early years following World War II. Yet while the United States and the Soviet Union both exploited the domestic conflicts in Greece and Iran in the late 1940s to further their own agendas, none of the great powers exploited unrest in Spain, Portugal, Piedmont, Sicily, or the German principalities in the early 1820s. Moreover, despite strong domestic pressure within parliament and among the political classes, Britain never sought to counter the Holy Alliance with a liberal common security arrangement, even after the ascendancy of the liberal faction in the 1820s. Consequently, despite the claim by many historians and political scientists that the bifurcation of the system after World War II was structurally inevitable, the case of nineteenth-century Europe suggests that it was not.[3] The theories proposed in this book suggest that one key difference was the great powers' commitment after the Napoleonic wars to their roles and responsibilities as security managers even in the face of other disagreements.

As a common security system, the Holy Alliance also demonstrated strong evidence of group cohesion. While the members disagreed on a number of issues, they remained committed to their special relationship and their common goals of providing for the collective defense of monarchy in Europe. This enabled historic rivals to place monarchic solidarity over territorial ambitions until the Crimean War in 1854. Neither Austria nor Prussia attempted to exploit the unrest within the German states in 1819 to increase their influence in central Europe at the expense of the other. Similarly, Russia remained loyal to the defense of monarchy even though it could have exploited the Hungarian rebellion against the Austrian empire in 1848 to weaken its potential rival.[4] By sending troops into Hungary to *crush* the rebellion rather than trying to profit from it, Russia acted within its role as a great power monarchy. This is contrary to what one would expect from a hegemonic competitor. It is not that the leaders of these states felt strong affections for each other. Rather they defined their security more in terms of protecting a transnational value—the survival of monarchy in Europe—than on increasing their power against each other.

Both these cases therefore support the hypothesis that the more states are committed to maintaining a particular set of interstate relationships, the more likely they will act as a member of that social group in international affairs according to group norms.

In analyzing the process through which amalgamated security communities were created in central and southern Europe, we saw a clear shift in how the relevant actors perceived themselves and their relations with the other principalities. More specifically, they began to define themselves as

Italians and Germans, rather than simply Tuscans, Piedmontese, Prussians, and Badans. At crucial moments the political leaders approached the important security issues from discernible Italian and German perspectives. This was even true of Bismarck, who has been traditionally portrayed as the quintessential realist politician. While he clearly favored the Prussian state over the German nation for much of his tenure, he ultimately understood that to be a Prussian in the mid-nineteenth century also meant being a German. This limited the degree to which he could promote a purely Prussian interest at the expense of the greater German community.

Thus in the Italian and German cases we saw examples of symbiosis—evidence of a strong positive identity—as the political elites of historically antagonistic states began to view themselves as members of a broader political community that extended beyond their borders. The transformation of central Europe and the Italian peninsula from balance of power systems to amalgamated security communities supports the thesis that under certain conditions states can redefine themselves and their interests in transnational terms.

The cases also support the hypothesis that transnational communities are most likely to form during and immediately following periods of social upheaval when domestic institutions are challenged, international orders undermined, and traditional structures eroded. Moreover, they support the proposition that states are more likely to act in a manner consistent with their transnational identities when their legitimacy is seriously challenged. In all three cases transnational communities were formed in the wake of social revolution and revolutionary challenges from domestic political actors. In chapter 3 the challenge was from the French revolution, which not only threatened absolute monarchy as a justification for rule but also undermined the dynastic system that had helped to provide a framework for interstate relations in Europe. I suggested that the great powers were able to relegitimize the European political system through the adoption of the legitimist principle and the institution of great power security management. This provided a positive standard from which state leaders could justify their rule to their domestic political classes and evaluate the intentions and actions of each other.

Both the Italian and German cases suggest that the challenge to the regimes' legitimacy following the revolutions of 1848 was the permissive condition that allowed the states to take the extraordinary act of annexing themselves to their traditional rivals. The kings and princes whose authority was based on historic succession lost their political base once constitution-

alism emerged as the dominant legitimizing principle. The newly empowered liberal revolutionaries sought legitimacy within the context of a national
state. At the same time, Italian and German nationalism was of a particular
kind. Unlike parochial forms, which would have highlighted the *distinctiveness* of Piedmont, Tuscany, Prussia, and Badan, it drew its strength from
transnational attachments that emphasized *similarities* between a diverse
group of states. Pan-nationalism was a transnational force that required the
elimination of the juridical borders that separated the populations.

Theoretical Implications

The preceding chapters suggest that while the concept of anarchy can be
useful for explaining some of the barriers to cooperation and systemic cohesion in international affairs, as a theoretical assumption it is too broad for
understanding the features and dynamics of an international or regional
order. The dramatic change in political relations between eighteenth- and
nineteenth-century Europe cannot be explained by the systemic ordering
principle, since politics in both centuries was conducted within an anarchic
environment. Moreover, the chapters also suggest that, as a variable, the
distribution of capabilities is indeterminate for predicting or explaining the
types of security arrangements that are created at a particular time. The
structure of the nineteenth-century European system was similar to that of
other eras, however the types of security arrangements developed by the great
powers differed considerably. Moreover, there was no evidence that any of
the security arrangements were derivative of structure. Neither polarity nor
hegemony can explain why these arrangements emerged during this particular period.

Until recently, the definition of international relations as the study of
egoistic competition in an unregulated environment set the terms of debate
in the literature. Thus, the "neorealist-neoliberal debate" has been primarily
concerned with the barriers to cooperation, the relative importance of wealth
verses security, and the degree to which institutions can ameliorate the
harsher aspects of anarchy.[5] As Robert Jervis points out, for neorealism (and,
I would add, institutionalism), the actors' values, preferences, beliefs, and
definition of self are all exogenous to the model and must be provided before
analysis can begin.[6] The preceding pages suggest that in doing so we miss
some crucial elements of international politics.

This book tried to address some of these missing pieces by showing how
definitions of self and other can influence and sometimes change the social

environment through which states interact. This supports the constructivist claim that there can be different types of anarchies. Once anarchy becomes a variable rather than a constant condition, we are freed from the assumption that rational egoism is necessarily the starting point of analysis. Thus there is a greater range of possible security arrangements, and other factors come into play in determining which is ultimately constructed during a particular period. Power is an important factor in understanding the range of options a given political actor can consider, yet it does not provide *grounds* for purposive or meaningful action, only the *means* to take action. Under some circumstances states may use power to forcibly attain specific ends at the expense of other states. In other situations states may use their power to facilitate more cohesive relations with selected states. As a result, power is also indeterminate.

This study contributes to a growing constructivist literature by showing through empirical examination that self-help and its consequences are not universal and unchanging results of anarchy. By focusing on how states can overcome the barriers created by anarchy rather than on the barriers themselves, the book supports the constructivist proposition that the international system is made rather than given. In highlighting the importance of intersubjective variables, in this case transnational identity, this study demonstrates the limits of a strictly materialist analysis. This suggests that much of what occurs in international relations cannot be explained by applying economistic, rational choice models. Rather, the application of sociological insights to the study of international politics can greatly expand the horizon of our field.

By showing how states can create cohesive security arrangements based on the idea of a common good, the book also helps to confirm the constructivist claim that preferences are influenced by social norms, social roles, and historically contingent discourse. Moreover, the empirical chapters showed many clear examples of how the interaction among state actors can change their self-perceptions. This supports the constructivist hypothesis that there is a direct positive correlation between what actors do and what they are. Until recently, most of these claims were based on theoretical argument. It is only in the past few years that attempts have been made to apply these insights to empirical cases.[7] The preceding pages help to strengthen these constructivist claims by examining cases that were hitherto within the sole province of realism, security studies.

In general, constructivist theories do not attempt to refute material and rationalist-based explanations as much as they seek to expand them. The empirical chapters support the wisdom of this approach. While identity was clearly a factor in each case, the study also confirms the role of power and interests in influencing the pattern of relationships and political choices that state officials make. As all three case chapters demonstrate, transnational communities are difficult to construct in part because a system that is based on mutually exclusive territorial units does breed competition. Moreover, the long histories of rivalry, mistrust, and conflict in interstate relations have cumulative and long-term effects.

In the absence of mitigating factors, anarchy can lead to a climate of uncertainty, and in security affairs the stakes are too high to allow for miscalculation.[8] Moreover, the institution of sovereignty reinforces a strong parochialism in domestic politics, which in turn exercises a strong force *against* transnational cohesion. Thus, even if anarchy does not constitute a single form with relatively fixed features, this does not mean that states can easily overcome their fears and parochialisms. In fact, even forward-looking and idealistic political leaders inevitably have conflicts between their international commitments and their domestic pressures. To the extent that domestic constituents believe that international politics is a zero-sum game, they are disinclined to extend their communities to include other societies. In this sense, the primary barrier to transnational community is not anarchy but sovereignty.

At the same time, ideational and material explanations are not necessarily incompatible. Structural variables can help account for the barriers to transnational community, while intersubjective ones can explain how these barriers can be transcended.[9] Both factors are present in the international environment. Realist and neorealist approaches, however, see structural constraints as a universal condition and cannot conceive of circumstances under which the barriers can be overcome to any significant degree. Constructivists try to articulate such circumstances, and the preceding pages justify this attempt. Both the theoretical and empirical chapters demonstrate how reflection and interaction among political actors can lead to a change in traditional roles.

The preceding chapters also confirm the utility of social identity theory and symbolic interactionist sociology as explanatory frameworks for understanding international politics. Both theories encourage international relations scholars to shift our focus from static structures to dynamic relationships. By using concepts derived from these approaches we are better able to explain the shift in thought and behavior that occurred during the nineteenth century. At the same time, the empirical evidence also disconfirms

Jonathan Mercer's interpretation of social identity theory as supporting the notion that self-help is inherent in an anarchic system. The present study draws from the same body of literature as Mercer, however, far from demonstrating that self-help is a universal and necessary consequence of intergroup relations in anarchy, it shows that states can and do form transnational communities among themselves.

The preceding pages demonstrate that recategorization and redefinitions of self do occur, leading to the formation of new types of social groups. Moreover, the evidence refutes Mercer's assumption that rivalry and suspicion is based on a state's need for a "positive social identity." On the contrary, as the empirical chapters show, states sometimes look *outside* their own societies in order to develop a positive identity through the creation of reference others. In the Italian and German cases the principalities drew their definitions of the nation to which they aspired to become from each other. Without the others, it would not have been possible to conceive of an Italian or German nation, since their own self-conceptions were firmly rooted in their parochial identities.

Similarly, the great powers, particularly the eastern monarchies, defined their roles and status from their unique relationships with each other. The transformation of Europe from a balance of power system to a concert system and common security arrangement required a form of self redefinition that could only emerge from consistent interaction.

Added Value and Future Research

Adding an additional explanatory factor to existing theories complicates our understanding of international politics. Chapter 1 tried to justify this move by discussing the limits of strictly material and rationalist explanations. Chapter 2 offered a theory for filling in the gaps. This placed a heavy burden on the empirical chapters to demonstrate its utility, since one could argue that the cases could be explained by alliance, cooperation, and institutional theories, without any reference to identity. The results of the study confirm the limitation of these explanations.

The two strongest realist theories for explaining the structure of security arrangements are found in the alliance and hegemony literature. Neither the Concert of Europe nor the Holy Alliance, however, fit the concept of an alliance, an institution whose primary purpose is to enhance state capabilities through combination with others in the face of a defined threat.[10] Nor was either arrangement the result of hegemony. Although some scholars such as Edward Gulick describe the post-Napoleon period as an example of "Europe's classical balance of power," neither the concert or the Holy Alliance acted as typical institutions in such a system. Rather than balancing the power of each other, the great powers *pooled* their power in order to collectively manage security affairs on the continent. The Holy Alliance was focused not on the power of other states but on two transnational movements, liberalism and nationalism, and they placed countervalues (continental monarchy and aristocracy) above self-aggrandizement.

While liberal institutionalists have generally avoided discussion of security institutions, one could still conceptualize both the concert and the Holy Alliance as regimes, without any reference to identity. There is a case to be made for this argument. Certainly states can cooperate to achieve mutual gains without sharing a common identity. Indeed, the appeal of institutionalist theories is their minimalism; they only require an overlapping interest to account for the creation of a regime. At the same time, the evidence presented in the cases suggest that this is insufficient for several reasons.

First, the level of commitment and cohesion required to maintain the concert and the Holy Alliance was far greater than that which can be explained by a simple regime. These institutions went beyond coordinating policies in given issue areas. They were based on the idea that there was some common good that superseded (and was not just consistent with) individual interest.[11] While regimes are reducible to the sum total of individual interest, chapter 3 suggests that the great power and monarchic communities each had an existence independent of its individual members. Both the concert and the alliance constituted social groups as defined in chapter 2, something that goes beyond regimes.

Second, the nature of the discourse suggests that the members also *viewed* themselves as constituting a unique group. The great powers and monarchs distinguished themselves as a group from the other states of Europe and spoke in terms that went beyond simple mutual interest. The norms and social roles were not only functional mechanisms for regulating behavior, they helped to create new categories of actors (great power monarchs) with expectations that went beyond those of other sovereign states.

Finally, the study suggests possibilities for future research. First, a deeper examination of domestic politics would provide a better understanding of the tension between transnational solidarity and domestic parochialism. This book focused primarily on systemic variables by examining how the interaction between state elites can lead to the development of transnational identities. To accomplish this, I held domestic politics constant by assuming that the elites of the ruling coalition represent the outcome of domestic political struggle. This was useful for examining the link between process and structure. Still, at least part of the variance in identity can be explained by this struggle and thus it would be useful to bring these processes into the picture. While chapter 4 did offer a greater focus on the internal dynamics of the German states, a more sustained study could only increase our knowledge.

Second, our understanding of transnational identities and the construction of cohesive security arrangements would benefit from a comparative study that examines cases where states sought to create transnational communities but failed. The empirical chapters examined three cases in which states successfully constructed cohesive security arrangements. This enabled me to trace the dynamics that led to the transformation of balance of power systems into community-based systems. However, now that the groundwork for studying transnational identity formation has been established, one can use these process variables to examine a wider range of cases. For example, why did the Italian state system successfully amalgamate in the nineteenth century but the Arab state system fail to do so in the twentieth? Why did the five great powers develop a common identity among themselves after the Napoleonic wars but fail to do so after World War I?

Implications for the Post–Cold War Order

If the type of transnational identity that is shared by a given group of states determines the type of security system they construct, we should be able to make broad predictions about future trends, given a specific set of conditions. While it is admittedly difficult to detect a community consciousness as it develops, we can find trends in patterns of thought and deed by using discourse analysis and an interpretation of behavior. All this leads to the proposition that if political leaders are conscious of their political attachments with other states they can make choices that either strengthen or weaken these attachments.

The end of the cold war unleashed widespread speculation by academics and political leaders about what the future of international politics would bring: instability or unprecedented global cooperation, internationalism or isolationism, sovereign equality or great power domination, world democratic revolution or old-fashioned despotism, a "New World order" or a return to pre–World War I hypernationalism. In the wake of the political upheavals that had occurred in Eastern Europe, many neorealists, for example, argue that the collapse of Soviet power and the accompanying end of bipolarity will undermine the delicate balance and stability that has prevented war in Europe since 1945.[12] Advocates of this position can point to the outbreak of war in the Balkans and Africa, tensions in the Middle East, and the ethnic conflicts sweeping many regions of the globe as indicative of political relations in the absence of central authority. They would thus predict the emergence of a new balance of power that reflects the structural conditions of the new order.

Taking a contrary position, neoliberals argue that as nations become increasingly locked into a series of complex interdependent relationships the fortunes of each state become tied to those of its neighbors.[13] Institutionalists hold that stability can be maintained through the construction of international institutions that stabilize domestic political structures and facilitate cooperation among states.[14] Robert Keohane and others are cautiously optimistic about this possibility, pointing out that many of the institutions constructed during the cold war are so deeply imbedded within the international system that they are likely to continue even in the face of other structural changes in the system.[15] They can support their arguments by pointing to the consolidation of the European Union and the unprecedented initiatives taken by the United Nations and other regional and international institutions toward stabilizing international politics.

Finally, liberal internationalists argue that with the ascendancy of liberal democracy as the dominant form of state organization in the world more states will resolve differences through international institutions under the rule of law. Arguing that the key variables are to be found at the domestic rather than the systemic level, Anne-Marie Burley holds that liberal states differ fundamentally from nonliberal ones and that these differences translate into different behavior patterns in the international realm. Thus, the different types of international cooperation depend upon the liberal/nonliberal distribution of the states within the system and on the specific contours of different issue agendas.[16]

This approach is consistent with the democratic peace thesis, which would predict that as the percentage of democracies in the world increase wars should be less frequent and relations more peaceful. Given this, the democratization of the major powers is the prerequisite for a cohesive collective security system. This position is strengthened by the fact that, despite the turmoil destabilizing many parts of the world, no democratic state has gone to war against another one.

What each of these scenarios have in common is its foundation in some type of structural or material variable: the distribution of capabilities, the presence or absence of institutions, and the distribution of liberal states, respectively. While structural factors will undoubtedly influence and constrain the behavior of states in the coming years, if the preceding analysis is correct, material factors in and of themselves are indeterminate. The nature of the interaction process and intersubjective perceptions of self and other must also be considered. Thus, one of the key variables in determining the direction of the post–cold war order will be the type or lack of transnational identities that form among states.

If peace among democracies is simply a natural outcome of domestic institutional structures, then war should eventually cease to be a feature of international politics as more states become democracies. However, if one views postwar liberal democracies as constituting a type of common security association, then the maintenance and expansion of this peace is dependent upon the development of stronger transnational identities among democratic states. A democratic state that identifies with other democratic states will view the world differently than one that sees the world from the vantage point of its regional identity, for example Europeanism or Asianism. Both are transnational identities, but each involves a different focus of loyalty. One sees the world in terms of democratic versus authoritarian and the other, for example, in terms of Asia versus North America. Democratic states can be nationalistic or regionalistic and may therefore not identify with other democratic states outside their region.

Common security associations form as mutual support systems for states choosing to promote a common value, usually in opposition to a counter-value. The ties between democracies were strongest when they could distinguish themselves as a group from authoritarian societies. Thus the historical fact that democracies have not gone to war against each other may not continue once democracy is no longer viewed as a distinguishing characteristic by political leaders. As more and more states begin to adopt democratic institutions, other differences—economic, social, ethnic—may take precedence. Consequently, there is no guarantee that a world of democracies would remain ideologically tied to one another, so long as other inequalities and differences remain.

The type of security arrangements that evolve over the next few years will likely define the nature of the post–cold war order in the coming period. The first and most obvious possibility is for the system to break down into competing blocs, ushering in a new balance of power. This outcome could be the result of domestic factors (for example, isolationist or nationalist forces within the government or society) or systemic ones (perceived threats from an ascending power such as China, Germany, or Japan). Under these conditions it would make little sense to discuss transnational communities or identities. If, however, political leaders choose to pursue alternatives to a balance of power system, there are at least three possibilities: (1) a concert model, based on the notion of great power management, (2) a collective security model, based on the concept of cosmopolitanism, and (3) regional cohesion based on pluralistic or amalgamated security communities. Each of these alternatives would represent a different type of transnational identity.

A modern-day concert based on an activist and interventionist U.N. Security Council would reinforce a great power identity and most likely lead to an international order in which stability is valued over justice.[17] Such an association would likely strengthen the ties between such identified states. As the Concert of Europe suggests, nations having a great power identity tend to internalize their role as managers and would therefore see their national interests as tied to the maintenance of a workable system of international governance. Thus international stability (although not necessarily peace) would likely be maintained; however, it would often be at the expense of a just settlement of national claims.[18] Kupchan and Kupchan suggest such an association, arguing that this "reflects current power realities" and would be "guided by Europe's major powers."[19]

As the history of the nineteenth century suggests, however, a modern-day concert could spark the emergence of opposition movements among (or within) the excluded powers by increasing and/or highlighting the distinction between the great powers and the secondary states. The Concert of Europe was able to successfully keep peace between the great powers for four decades, however, while major war did not occur, domestic rebellions were common throughout the period. This opposition culminated in the European-wide revolutions of 1848, which ultimately destroyed the Vienna system. One lesson that can be learned from the nineteenth-century concert is that obligations cannot be imposed on a society of states by a small number of great powers indefinitely.

A modern-day league of nations system (based on collective security rather than great power management) could strengthen ties among all sovereign states and lead to a greater transnational identity based on cosmopolitanism within the community of nations. This type of cosmopolitan identity would view all states that accepted basic values and principles (as defined by the United Nations and other institutions) as constituting a single international community. The self-other distinction would be made on the basis of those who adhered to these principles and those who did not, for example, peaceful versus aggressive states. This is the type of approach that many United Nations enthusiasts have been striving for.[20]

If such a system persisted over time, it would strengthen the political and normative bonds between the individual states and the broader international community. This would not mean unanimity or harmony, but rather a commitment toward maintaining a cohesive system based on a common set of goals and a common good. The key factor is whether cooperating states perceive themselves as constituting a community. Practically speaking, this type of arrangement could only work if most states commit themselves to the rules and principles of international society. Such an arrangement would likely value the application of universal principles (justice) along with the maintenance of stability and order.

At the same time, an identification with a "community" based on a particular set of universal principles could also foster exclusion of those who do not share in these principles (the so-called pariah states). For example, those nations that did not adhere to the community's definition of "human rights" could find themselves excluded from the institutions of international society. As realist theorists point out, universal principles are often defined and imposed by the most powerful states and are often a mask for self-interest.[21] In these cases it could threaten the cohesion of the community. For this reason a collective security system cannot be imposed by hegemonic powers. It could only work in the long term if its underlying principles truly reflected the community of states as a whole, even if the great powers provided the resources for enforcement.

The emergence and/or maintenance of pluralistic or amalgamated security communities could stabilize regional political relations by strengthening ties among states within cognitive regions. As suggested above, PSCs reduce relative gains concerns and foster group cohesion, which can lead to demilitiarization and close cooperation. If such communities were to develop within Latin America and Asia and be maintained within North America and Europe, regional disputes would not likely escalate into international conflicts. The institutional structures already exist for facilitating these types of arrangements, for example, the Organization of American States and the Association of South East Asian Nations. Amalgamated security communities would further consolidate interstate relations by reducing the number of borders that separate societies.

As demonstrated both theoretically and in the empirical cases, community-based security arrangements are difficult to construct, and the formation of transnational identities are challenged by the institution of sovereignty. Cohesive security systems could easily be thwarted by a refusal of key states to fully participate in the kinds of international associations that could strengthen transnational identities. However, if states tend to act on the basis of how they define their situations and the way they view themselves in relations to others, political leaders can also make choices about the type of world in which they wish to live.

For example, whether the United States acts like a Gilpinian hegemon, a Waltzian great power, or a leader in a Wilsonian international community of states depends not only on its resource capabilities but also on how it chooses to define its role in the world.[22] This in turn is affected by the way it *acts* toward other states. At the same time, even if the political elites of the key states are committed to constructing a cohesive transnational political community, domestic interest groups or opposition political leaders can undermine the foundation for state participation. In this case domestic politics would be a more important variable in determining the outcome than systemic factors.

Rival power blocks could form if states take actions and create associations that are clearly exclusionary in design and form. This is why it is important for political leaders to carefully consider the types of institutions they construct. Western institutions have been highly successful in creating a sense of group cohesion among Western states, and, as a result, it is unlikely that a revival of traditional rivalries and animosities would develop within Western Europe and North America. However, a narrowing as opposed to a broadening of these institutions could create and institutionalize a West-Rest cleavage, with serious security consequences. This could unnecessarily help to bring about Samuel Huntington's "clash of civilizations."[23]

For example, if NATO becomes more active as a common security institution but continually acts unilaterally in opposition to more inclusive institutions, it can reinforce unnecessary distinctions between Western and non-Western societies. Russia has already demonstrated strong reactions to NATO's role in providing security management for Europe at its expense. If this trend continues, NATO can emerge as a negative reference group among powerful domestic actors, prompting calls for more confrontational policies.

To the extent that transnational identities and transnational communities facilitate cohesive relationships and foster greater cooperation between states, they can be viewed as positive. In practice, however, they could produce outcomes that many people would find objectionable. For example, while the Holy Alliance helped the Eastern powers to overcome their historic conflicts by creating a foundation for group solidarity, it also impeded progress by undermining the many reforms initiated by the French revolution. Few people currently view the collective defense of monarchy as a positive historical development. Henry Kissinger's portrayal of Metternich as a great statesman would look different from the vantage point of a leader in the German reform movement of 1819.

This points to one of the dangers of using identity theories as a foundation for developing practical policies. To the extent that transnational identities help to diminish the conceptual boundaries that divide societies, they can lead to a more cohesive, stable system. However, if they are used to create new boundaries, they can produce fresh animosities and new conflicts. The conceptual division of the world into the civilized and uncivilized during the colonial period was used by political leaders to justify highly exploitative and conflictual practices toward non-European societies.[24] Transnationalism, in this case helped to *create* new conflicts. Similarly, Samuel Huntington's search for an external enemy in order to create a new sense of purpose within the West is a modern application of this principle.[25] Yet, as this book has demonstrated, inclusionary associations could deemphasize distinctions based on ethnicity, culture, economic status, or region just as exclusionary ones could make them more pronounced. In this sense, the future is in our hands.

Notes

1. The Concept of Transnational Communities

1. An important exception is Emanual Adler and Michael Barnett, *Security Communities* (Cambridge: Cambridge University Press, 1998).

2. See Robert O. Keohane, *After Hegemony: Cooperation and Discord in the World Political Economy* (Princeton: Princeton University Press, 1984), especially pp. 51–57.

3. See Robert MacIver, *On Community, Society, and Power: Selected Writings*, ed. Leon Bramson (Chicago: University of Chicago Press, 1970).

4. Ferdinand Tönnies, for example, holds that communities are tied to a form of kinship and cannot be self-consciously built or instituted. See his *Community and Society (Gemeinschaft und Gesellschaft)*, trans. and ed. Charles P. Loomis (New York: Harper and Row, 1957).

5. Jean-Jacques Rousseau, *The Social Contract and Discourses*, trans. G. D. H. Cole (New York: Dutton, 1950).

6. The common use of the concept transnational in the literature has been to describe relations among political actors other than states, for example nongovernmental organizations, social movements, and bureaucratic agencies from different governments. There is no reason, however, why state officials cannot also conceive of themselves and their societies as belonging to a broader community beyond their juridical borders. For a sample of recent literature on transnationalism as nongovernmentalism, see Thomas Risse-Kappen, *Bringing Transnational Relations Back In: Non-State Actors, Domestic Structures, and International Institutions* (Cambridge: Cambridge University Press, 1995); and Kathryn Sikkink, "Human Rights, Principled Issue Networks, and Sovereignty in Latin America," *International Organization*,

vol. 47, no. 3 (Summer 1993), pp. 411–42). See also Robert Keohane and Joseph Nye, eds., *Transnational Relations and World Politics* (Cambridge: Harvard University Press, 1971); and James Rosenau, *The Study of Global Interdependence: Essays on the Transnationalization of World Affairs* (London: Frances Pinter, 1980).

7. See *The American Heritage Dictionary*, 2d. college ed. (Boston: Houghton Miffin, 1985), p. 639.

8. Waltz argues that "to the extent that dynamics of a system limit the freedom of its units, their behavior and the outcomes of their behavior become predictable . . . (therefore) systems theories explain why different units behave similarly and, despite their variations, produce outcomes that fall within expected ranges." Kenneth Waltz, *Theory of International Politics* (New York: Random House, 1979), p. 72.

9. E. H. Carr, *The Twenty Years' Crisis, 1919–1939* (New York: Harper and Row, 1964 [1939]), p. 89.

10. See Kenneth Waltz, "Realist Thought and Neorealist Theory," *Journal of International Affairs*, vol. 44, no. 1, pp. 21–37.

11. Robert Art and Robert Jervis, "The Meaning of Anarchy," in Robert Art and Robert Jervis, eds., *International Politics: Anarchy, Force, Political Economy and Decision Making* (Boston: Little, Brown, 1985), p. 3.

12. See Robert Gilpin, *War and Change in World Politics* (Cambridge: Cambridge University Press, 1981), p. 7.

13. Keohane, *After Hegemony*. Stephen Krasner defines an international regime as a set of principles, norms, rules, and decision-making procedures around which actor expectations converge in a given issue area. "Structural Causes and Regime Consequences: Regimes as Intervening Variables," in Stephen Krasner, ed., *International Regimes* (Ithaca: Cornell University Press, 1983), p. 1.

14. Robert Axelrod and Robert Keohane, "Achieving Cooperation Under Anarchy: Strategies and Institutions," *World Politics*, no. 38 (October 1985), pp. 226–54.

15. This line of argument was refined and popularized in international relations by Alexander Wendt in "Anarchy is What States Make of It: The Social Construction of Power Politics," *International Organization*, vol. 46, no. 2 (Spring 1992). For an excellent analysis of the origins and development of constructist research programs, see John Ruggie, "Introduction: What Makes the World Hang Together?" in his *Constructing the World Polity: Essays on International Institutionalization* (New York: Routledge, 1998). For a sample of other constructivist literature, see Nicholas Onuf, *World of Our Making: Rules and Rule in Social Theory and International Relations* (Columbia: University of South Carolina Press, 1989); Alexander Wendt, "Collective Identity Formation and the International State," *American Political Science Review*, vol. 88 (June 1994); Peter Katzenstein, ed., *The Culture of National Security: Norms and Identity in World Politics* (New York: Columbia University Press, 1996); and Martha Finnemore, *The National Interest in International Society* (Ithaca: Cornell University Press, 1996).

16. Intersubjectivity refers to the shared symbolic meanings that actors assign to

particular situations. Unlike objective definitions—which are exogenously given—or subjective ones—which are endogenously developed by individual actors—intersubjective meanings are perceptions that are shared by at least two actors. They are developed in the process of communication and interaction. I discuss this process in greater detail in chapter 2.

17. Wendt, "Anarchy Is What States Make of It."

18. Ibid.

19. Barry Buzan makes a similar point in Barry Buzan, Charles Jones, and Richard Little, *The Logic of Anarchy* (New York: Columbia University Press, 1993), section 1.

20. David Dessler, "What's at Stake in the Agent-Structure Debate?" *International Organization*, vol. 43 (Summer 1989), pp. 455–56.

21. Robert Keohane defines institutions as both a general pattern or categorization of activity and a particular human-constructed arrangement, formally or informally organized. He also argues that specific institutions can be defined in terms of their rules, although he is referring to regulative, rather than constitutive, rules. Robert Keohane, "International Institutions: Two Approaches," in his *International Institutions and State Power: Essays in International Relations Theory* (Boulder: Westview, 1989), pp. 162–63.

22. See Joseph R. Strayer and Dana C. Munro, *The Middle Ages, 395–1500* (New York: Appleton-Century-Crofts, 1970).

23. The definition of sovereignty as constitutional independence is from Alan James, *Sovereign Statehood: The Basis of International Society* (Boston: Allen and Unwin, 1986).

24. See Benjamin Miller, "Explaining the Emergence of Great Power Concerts," *Review of International Studies*, vol. 20, no. 4 (October 1994), p. 329.

25. Two of the best works on the concert as a system are Richard Elrod, "The Concert of Europe: A Fresh Look at an International System," *World Politics*, vol. 28 (January 1976); and Robert Jervis, "From Balance to Concert: A Study in International Security Cooperation," in Kenneth A. Oye, ed., *Cooperation Under Anarchy* (Princeton: Princeton University Press, 1986).

26. I use the term *common* to distinguish them from *collective* security systems.

27. See Karl Deutsch et al., *Political Community and the North Atlantic Area: International Organization in the Light of Historical Experience* (Princeton: Princeton University Press, 1957).

28. Ibid., p. 58.

29. This definition is loosely adapted from Deutsch et al., who coined the term and conceptualized this type of security arrangement. See their *Political Community in the North Atlantic Area*. For recent work on this topic, see Adler and Barnett, *Security Communities*.

30. There is a vast literature on collective security and its institutions. The classic works include Arnold Wolfers, *Discord and Collaboration: Essays on International*

Politics (Baltimore: Johns Hopkins University Press, 1988), chapters 11 and 12; Hans Morganthau, *Politics Among Nations: The Struggle for Power and Peace* (New York: McGraw-Hill, 1993), chapter 19; Kenneth Thompson, "Collective Security Reexamined, *American Political Science Review*, vol. 47, no. 3 (September 1953); Inis Claude, *Swords into Plowshares* (New York: Random House, 1971), chapter 12; and Roland Stromberg, "The Idea of Collective Security," *Journal of the History of Ideas*, vol. 17, no. 2 (April 1956). For more recent treatments, see Charles A. Kupchan and Clifford A. Kupchan, "Concerts, Collective Security, and the Future of Europe," *International Security*, vol. 16, no. 1 (Summer 1991), p. 155; and Richard K. Betts, "Systems of Peace or Causes of War?" *International Security*, vol. 17, no. 1 (Summer 1992). Other recent articles include John Mueller, "A New Concert of Europe?" *Foreign Policy*, vol. 77 (Winter 1988–1990); James E. Goodby, "A New European Concert," *Arms Control Today* vol. 21, no. 1 (January/February 1991); and Gregory Flynn and David Scheffer, "Limited Collective Security," *Foreign Policy*, vol. 80 (Fall 1990).

31. There is a vast literature on the relationship between democracy and peace, dating back to the work of Immanual Kant. Some of the recent work takes this a step further by arguing that democratic states share a unique relationship among themselves that can be loosely viewed as a community. See, for example, Anne Marie Slaughter, "Toward an Age of Liberal Nations," *Harvard International Law Journal*, vol. 33, no. 2 (Spring 1992), and "Law Among Liberal States: Liberal Internationalism and the Act of State Doctrine," *Columbia Law Review*, vol. 92, no. 8 (December 1992). For a good articulation of the democratic peace thesis, see the articles by Doyle, Russett, and Owen in Michael Brown, Sean Lynn-Jones, and Steven Miller, eds., *Debating the Democratic Peace* (Cambridge: MIT Press, 1993).

32. Constitutive variables create and revise the actors or interests which agent-oriented approaches take for granted. See Alexander Wendt, *Social Theory of International Politics* (Cambridge: Cambridge University Press, forthcoming).

33. For a similar argument on the constitutive nature of norms, see Friedrich Kratochwil and John Ruggie, "International Organization: A State of the Art or an Art of the State?" *International Organization*, vol. 40 (August 1986), pp. 753–75.

34. See Quentin Skinner, *The Foundation of Modern Political Thought*, vol. 2 (Cambridge: Cambridge University Press, 1978), p. 352.

35. See, for example, Stephen Krasner, "Westphalia and All That," in Judith Goldstein and Robert Keohane, eds., *Ideas and Foreign Policy: Beliefs, Institution, and Political Change* (Ithaca: Cornell University Press, 1994); and Marcus Fischer, "Feudal Europe, 800–1300: Communal Discourse and Conflictual Practices," *International Organization*, vol. 46, no. 2 (Spring 1992), pp. 427–66.

36. For an excellent challenge to the assumption-of-interests approach, see Martha Finnemore, *National Interests in International Society* (Ithaca: Cornell University Press, 1996).

37. Alexander Wendt makes a similar suggestion in "Identity and Structural

Change in International Politics," in Yosef Lapid and Friedrich Kratochwil, eds., *The Return of Culture and Identity in IR Theory* (Boulder: Rienner, 1996), p. 52.

2. Transnational Identities and International Politics

1. For a good discussion of how rules can motivate and generate behavior, see David Dessler, "What's at Stake in the Agent-Structure Debate?" *International Organization*, vol. 43 (Summer 1989), pp. 441–73.

2. John Hewitt, *Self and Society: A Symbolic Interactionist Social Psychology* (Boston: Allyn and Bacon, 1976), p. 109.

3. For an excellent comparison of the similarities and differences in these theories, see Michael Hogg, Deborah Terry, and Katherine White, "A Tale of Two Theories: A Critical Comparison of Identity Theory with Social Identity Theory," *Social Psychology Quarterly*, vol. 58., no. 4 (1995), pp. 255–69.

4. Social identity theory developed from an attempt to provide an alternative to the assertion that intergroup conflict is by definition characterized by some real competition for scarce resources. For a sample of this literature, see Henri Tajfel, ed., *Social Identity and Intergroup Relations* (Cambridge: Cambridge University Press, 1982); John Turner, *Rediscovering the Social Group* (New York: Blackwell, 1987); Michael Hogg and Dominic Abrams, *Social Identifications: A Social Psychology of Intergroup Relations and Group Process* (New York: Routledge, 1988); and Dominic Abrams and Michael A. Hogg, *Social Identity Theory: Constructive and Critical Advances* (New York: Springer-Verlag, 1990).

5. Jonathan Mercer, "Anarchy and Identity," *International Organization*, vol. 49, no. 2 (Spring 1995), p. 251.

6. Ibid., p. 246.

7. Ibid., p. 233.

8. Symbolic internationalism grew from the work of George Herbert Mead, although it also has roots in German idealism, Scottish moralism, and American pragmatism. It was further developed by Herbert Blumer, particularly in his *Symbolic Interactionism: Perspective and Method* (Englewood Cliffs, N.J.: Prentice Hall, 1969). See also Erving Goffman, *The Presentation of Self in Everyday Life* (Garden City, N.J.: Doubleday Anchor, 1959); Tamotsu Shibutani, "Reference Groups as Perspectives," *American Journal of Sociology*, vol. 60, pp. 562–69; Sheldon Stryker, *Symbolic Interactionism: A Social Structural Version* (Menlo Park, Cal.: Benjamin/Cummings, 1980); and Joel M. Charon, *Symbolic Interactionism: An Introduction, an Interpretation, an Integration Method* (Englewood Cliffs, N.J.: Prentice Hall, 1979).

9. Hewitt, *Self and Society*, p. 115.

10. Charon, *Symbolic Interactionism*, p. 24.

11. Stephen Krasner, for example, argues that the kinds of institutionalizing mechanisms that can work so powerfully to socialize individuals in domestic polities are not available on the international level. See his "Compromising Westphalia,"

International Security, vol. 20, no. 3 (Winter 1995), p. 149. This assumption can also be found in Kenneth Waltz, *Theory of International Politics* (New York: Random House, 1979); and Hans Morganthau, *Politics Among Nations: The Struggle for Power and Peace* (New York: McGraw-Hill, 1993).

12. Stryker, *Symbolic Interactionism*, p. 79; Hogg and Abrams, *Social Identifications*, p. 26.

13. Hedley Bull argues that a society of states exists in the sense that the participants are conscious of certain common interests and common values and conceive themselves to be bound by a common set of rules and institutions in their relations with one another. See *The Anarchical Society: A Study of Order in World Politics* (New York: Columbia University Press, 1977), especially chapters 1 and 2.

14. Alex Wendt makes a case for the possibility of this deeper transformation, although this would require a more fundamental change than that which will be addressed in this book. See Alexander Wendt, "Anarchy Is What States Make of It: The Social Construction of Power Politics," *International Organization*, vol. 46, no. 2 (Spring 1992).

15. See Michael Barnett, "Institutions, Roles, and Disorder: The Case of the Arab States System," *International Studies Quarterly*, vol. 37 (1993), pp. 274.

16. This is similar to the definition proposed by Gianfranco Poggi, *The Development of the Nation-State: A Sociological Introduction* (Stanford: Stanford University Press, 1978), p. 1.

17. There is a large literature from a variety of perspectives on the relative autonomy of the state vis-à-vis society. See, for example, Peter Evans, Dietrich Rueschemeyer, and Theda Skocpol, eds., *Bringing the State Back In* (Cambridge: Cambridge University Press, 1985); Michael Mann, "The Autonomous Power of the State: Its Origins, Mechanisms, and Results," in John Hall, ed., *States in History* (New York: Blackwell), pp. 109–36; and Alfred Stepan, *The State and Society: Peru in Comparative Perspective* (Princeton: Princeton University Press, 1978). In international relations this position is held by, among others, Stephen Krasner, *Defending the National Interest: Raw Materials Investments and U.S. Foreign Policy* (Princeton: Princeton University Press, 1978).

18. See Stepan, *State and Society*, p. xii.

19. "Ruling coalition" refers not to the government but to the combination of social forces (for example, labor, business, church) that dominate the state apparatus.

20. Robert Gilpin conceives of the state as a coalition of coalitions whose objectives and interests result from the bargaining among the several coalitions composing the larger society and political elite. See his *War and Change in World Politics* (Cambridge: Cambridge University Press, 1981), p. 19.

21. Theda Skocpol, "Bringing the State Back In: Strategies of Analysis in Current Research," in Evans, Rueschemeyer, and Skocpol, *Bringing the State Back In*, p. 9.

22. See Michael Hogg, *The Social Psychology of Group Cohesiveness: From Attraction to Social Identity* (New York: New York University Press, 1992), p. 90.

23. Mead's primary work dealing with issues of self and society was published from a series of lectures in George Herbert Mead, *Mind, Self, and Society from the Standpoint of a Social Behaviorist*, ed. Charles W. Morris (Chicago: University of Chicago Press, 1934).

24. Mead, *Mind, Self, and Society*, pp. 138–140.

25. As Hegel argues, "Self-consciousness achieves its satisfaction only in another self-consciousness." G. W. F. Hegel, *Phenomenology of Spirit*, trans. A. V. Miller (New York: Oxford University Press, 1977), p. 110, par. 175.

26. Hewitt, *Self and Society*, p. 101.

27. Mead, *Mind, Self and Society*, p. 135.

28. G. W. F. Hegel, *Philosophy of Right*, trans. T. M. Knox (New York: Oxford University Press, 1967), p. 38, section 40. Also see translator's note, p. 320.

29. Alex Wendt argues, for example, that the signals exchanged during "first contacts" are crucial in helping actors to define a situation as threatening or benign. See "Anarchy Is What States Make of It," p. 405.

30. Mead, *Mind, Self, and Society*; Hewitt, *Self and Society*, pp. 77–82.

31. John Hewitt refers to this as "typification." See his *Self and Society*, pp. 122–24. See also Alfred Schultz, *On Phenomenology and Social Relations* (Chicago: University of Chicago Press, 1970), pp. 11–122.

32. Shibutani, "Reference Groups as Perspectives, pp. 562–69.

33. Anthony Giddens, *The Nation-State and Violence* (Berkeley: University of California Press), p. 263.

34. See, for example, Jeremy Black, *The Rise of the European Powers* (New York: Routledge, Chapman and Hall, 1990), pp. 150–54.

35. There is a large literature examining how these boundaries are constructed. For a sample of the various approaches, see Walker Connor, *Ethnonationalism: The Quest for Understanding* (Princeton: Princeton University Press, 1994); Anthony D. Smith, *The Ethnic Origin of Nations* (Oxford: Oxford University Press, 1986); Ernest Gellner, *Nations and Nationalism* (Ithaca: Cornell University Press, 1983); Benedict Anderson, *Imagined Communities: Reflections on the Origins and Spread of Nationalism* (London: Verso, 1983); and John Breuilly, *Nationalism and the State* (Chicago: University of Chicago Press, 1982).

36. T. A. Elliot, *Us and Them: A Study in Group Consciousness* (Aberdean: Aberdean University Press, 1986).

37. See Hugh Seton-Watson, *Nations and States: An Enquiry Into the Origins of Nations and the Politics of Nationalism* (London: Methuen, 1977).

38. See E. J. Hobsbawm, *Nations and Nationalism Since 1780: Programme, Myth, Reality* (Cambridge: Cambridge University Press, 1990), chapter 1.

39. See David Armstrong, *Revolution and World Order: The Revolutionary State in International Society* (Oxford: Clarendon, 1983), chapter 4.

40. Donald Puchala and Raymond Hopkins's study on colonialism clearly demonstrates the importance of the civilized-uncivilized distinction in legitimizing im-

perial practices. See "International Regimes: Lessons from Inductive Analysis," in Stephen D. Krasner, ed., *International Regimes* (Ithaca: Cornell University Press, 1983), p. 70.

41. Hogg and Abrams, *Social Identifications*, p. 25.

42. Stryker, *Symbolic Interactionism*, p. 61.

43. A social group is defined as two or more actors who share a common identification and perceive themselves to be members of the same social category. See John Turner, "Toward a Cognitive Redefinition of the Social Group," in Henri Tajfel, ed., *Social Identity and Intergroup Relations* (Cambridge: Cambridge University Press, 1982), p. 15.

44. This is the basic theme of the "democratic peace" literature. See chapter 1, note 31.

45. For an excellent analysis of negative interdependence, see Albert O. Hirschman, *National Power and the Structure of Foreign Trade* (Berkeley: University of California Press, 1945).

46. Jonathan Turner, Michael Hogg, P. Oakes, S. Reichter, and M. Wetherell, *Rediscovering the Social Group: A Self-Categorization Theory* (New York: Blackwell, 1987.

47. For an extended discussion of the link between process and identity, see Wendt, "Anarchy Is What States Make of It."

48. As Robert Jervis points out, the shared experience of fighting a winning war produces significant ties between allies. These allies form the core of the concert system. See his "From Balance to Concert: A Study of International Security Cooperation," in Kenneth A. Oye, ed., *Cooperation Under Anarchy* (Princeton: Princeton University Press, 1986), pp. 60–61.

49. Mead, *Mind, Self and Society*, pp. 155–58.

50. See Anthony Giddens, *Central Problems in Social Theory: Action, Structure, and Contradiction in Social Analysis* (London: Macmillan, 1979), p. 117.

51. Hewitt, *Self and Society*, p. 101.

52. Kal Holsti, "National Role Conceptions in the Study of Foreign Policy," *International Studies Quarterly*, vol. 14 (1970), pp. 245–46.

53. Anne-Marie Burley argues, for example, that liberal states tend to hold each other to a different standard than that for nonliberal regimes. Thus, for states to enter the club of liberal nations, they are expected to follow certain norms in choosing their governments and in their foreign relations. See her "Law Among Liberal States: Liberal Internationalism and the Act of State Doctrine," in *Columbia Law Review*, vol. 92, no. 8 (December 1992), p. 1913.

54. See Giddens, *Central Problems in Social Theory*, pp. 118–19; and Stryker, *Symbolic Interactionism*, p. 73.

55. Stryker, *Symbolic Interactionism*, p. 68.

56. Jack Snyder argues, for example, that European institutions help to facilitate democratization in Eastern Europe by providing such a standard. See his "Averting

Anarchy in the New Europe," *International Security*, vol. 14, no. 4 (Spring 1990), pp. 5–41.

57. Michael Barnett, "Sovereignty, Nationalism, and Regional Order in the Arab States System," *International Organization*, vol. 49, no. 3 (Summer 1995), pp. 479–510.

3. A Great Power Concert and a Community of Monarchs

1. Alan Sked, "The Metternich System, 1815–1848," in Alan Sked, ed., *Europe's Balance of Power, 1815–1848* (London: Macmillan, 1979), p. 98.

2. Historians and political scientists date the life of these systems in a variety of ways, depending upon how they characterize them. The congress system declined after 1823 when Britain decided not to continue attending, although great power congresses continued to be held through the end of the century. However the system of collective great power consultation, cooperation, and management that characterized the Concert of Europe lasted until the Crimean War in 1854. See, for example, Richard Elrod, "The Concert of Europe: A Fresh Look at an International System," *World Politics*, vol. 28 (January 1976) and Gordon Craig and Alexander George, *Force and Statecraft: Diplomatic Problems of Our Time* (New York: Oxford University Press, 1995), chapter 3. Hajo Holborn goes further, arguing that the system of collective management and consultation lasted until the First World War. Hajo Holborn, *The Political Collapse of Europe* (New York: Knopf, 1966), p. 27. The Metternich system lasted until the European revolutions of 1848.

3. See Jeremy Black, *The Rise of the European Powers, 1679–1793* (New York: Routledge, Chapman and Hall, 1990).

4. Harold Nicholson, *Congress of Vienna: A Study in Allied Unity, 1812–1822* (New York: Harcourt, Brace, 1946) p. 28; Walter Alison Phillips, *The Confederation of Europe: Study of the European Alliance, 1813–1823* (London: Longmans, Green, 1920), p. 98.

5. Paul W. Schroeder, "Containment Nineteenth-Century Style: How Russia Was Restrained," *South Atlantic Quarterly* vol. 82, no. 1 (Winter 1983), p. 1.

6. Waltz argues that "if we observe outcomes that the theory leads us to expect even though strong forces work against them, the theory will begin to command belief." Kenneth Waltz, *Theory of International Politics* (New York: Random House, 1979), p. 125.

7. Robert Jervis, "From Balance to Concert: A Study of International Security Cooperation," in Kenneth A. Oye, ed., *Cooperation Under Anarchy* (Princeton: Princeton University Press, 1986), pp. 60–61.

8. Ibid., p. 67.

9. See Robert Axelrod, *The Evolution of Cooperation* (New York: Basic, 1984); and Robert Axelrod and Robert Keohane, "Achieving Cooperation Under Anarchy: Strategies And Institutions," *World Politics*, vol. 38 (October 1985), pp. 226–54.

10. Charles Kupchan and Clifford Kupchan, "Concerts, Collective Security, and the Future of Europe," *International Security*, vol. 16, no. 1 (Summer 1991); Richard Rosecrance, *Action and Reaction in World Politics: International Systems in Perspective* (Boston: Little, Brown, 1963), p. 56; Benjamin Miller, "Explaining the Emergence of Great Power Concerts," *Review of International Studies*, vol. 20, no. 4; Hedley Bull, *The Anarchical Society: A Study of Order in World Politics* (New York: Columbia University Press, 1977), pp. 225–27.

11. Paul Schroeder, *The Transformation of European Politics, 1763–1848* (New York: Oxford University Press, 1994), p. vii.

12. See, for example, Gordon Craig and Alexander George, *Force and Statecraft: Diplomatic Problems of Our Time* (New York: Oxford University Press, 1995), chapter 3; and Henry Kissinger, *A World Restored: Metternich, Castlereagh, and the Problems of Peace, 1812–1822* (Boston: Houghton Mifflin, 1959).

13. Robert Gilpin, *War and Change in World Politics* (Cambridge: Cambridge University Press, 1981), chapter 5.

14. There are numerous political/historical works examining the impact of the French revolution on the ancien régime. Three classics include Albert Sorel, *Europe and the French Revolution: The Political Tradition of the Old Régime*, trans. Alfred Cobban and J. W. Hunt (Fontana Library, 1969 [1885]); Alexis de Tocqueville, *The Old Régime and the French Revolution* (New York: Anchor, 1955); and E. J. Hobsbawm, *The Age of Revolution: 1789–1848* (New York: New American Library, 1962).

15. See Stephen Holmes, "Two Concepts of Legitimacy: France After the Revolution," *Political Theory*, vol. 10, no. 2 (May 1982), p. 166.

16. See, for example, Robert Gildea, *Barricades and Borders: Europe 1800–1914* (Oxford: Oxford University Press, 1987), p. 61.

17. Hobsbawm, *The Age of Revolution*, p. 114.

18. Guglielmo Ferrero, *The Reconstruction of Europe: Talleyrand and the Congress of Vienna, 1814–1815* (New York: Putnam, 1941), p. 141.

19. Enno Kraehe describes the situation as "unrest in the kaleidoscopic world of the third Germany [the territories apart from Prussia and Austria] where millions of 'souls' waited uneasily from one day to the next wondering where new boundaries would be drawn and who their new sovereigns would be." See Enno E. Kraehe, *Metternich's German Policy* (Princeton: Princeton University Press, 1983), p. 18.

20. Michael Broers argues that the deepest, most intractable problem facing the majority of governments in the early nineteenth century was the legacy of the revolution, particularly how governments could make themselves respected and how newly restored rulers would prove themselves to their subjects. See his *Europe After Napoleon: Revolution, Reaction, and Romanticism, 1814–1848* (Manchester: Manchester University Press, 1996), particularly p. 15.

21. Report from Talleyrand to King Louis during his journey from Ghent to Paris, Duc de Broglie, ed., *The Memoirs of the Prince de Talleyrand* (New York: Putnam, 1891), vol. 3, p. 147.

22. Guillaume de Bertier de Sauvigny, *The Bourbon Restoration* (Philadelphia: University of Pennsylvania Press, 1966), p. 57.

23. Andreas Osiander, *The States System of Europe, 1640–1990: Peacemaking and the Conditions of International Stability* (Oxford: Clarendon, 1994), p. 232.

24. Osiander (ibid.) argues that the balance of power was the primary outcome of Utrecht. While he holds that dynastic legitimacy was not institutionalized until after Vienna, others such as David Armstrong and E. N. Williams, argue that it provided the foundation for the eighteenth century European order. See David Armstrong, *Revolution and World Order: The Revolutionary State in International Society* (Oxford: Clarendon, 1993), p. 89; and E. N. Williams, *The Ancien Régime in Europe: Government and Society in the Major States, 1648–1789* (London: Penguin, 1988 [1970]).

25. Jeremy Black, *The Rise of the European Powers* (New York: Routledge, Chapman and Hall, 1990), p. 150.

26. Derek McKay and H. M. Scott, *The Rise of the Great Powers, 1648–1815* (London and New York: Longman, 1983), p. 210.

27. Osiander, *The States System of Europe*; and Paul Schroeder, "The Transformation of Political Thinking, 1787–1848," in Jack Snyder and Robert Jervis, eds., *Coping with Complexity in the International System* (Boulder: Westview, 1993).

28. Sir Charles Webster, *The Congress of Vienna, 1814–1815* (London: Thames and Hudson, 1934), p. 21; Schroeder, *The Transformation of European Politics*, chapters 10 and 11.

29. In 1810 Spain, most of Italy, the Confederation of the Rhine, and the Grand Duchy of Warsaw were considered satellites. Russia, Prussia, and Austria were either occupied by, allied to, or forced into an alliance with Napoleon. See McKay and Scott, *The Rise of the Great Powers*, map 8, pp. 368–69.

30. See H. G. Schenk, *The Aftermath of the Napoleonic Wars: The Concert of Europe, an Experiment* (New York: Howard Fertig, 1967), p. 120.

31. Quoted in Guillaume de Bertier de Sauvigny, *Metternich and His Times* (London: Darton, Longmann and Todd, 1962), p. 161.

32. C. A. Macartney, *The Hapsburg Empire, 1790–1918* (London: Widenfeld and Nicholson, 1969), p. 191.

33. Schroeder, *The Transformation of European Politics*, p. 527.

34. Schenk, *The Aftermath of the Napoleonic Wars*; Kissinger, *A World Restored*; and Schroeder, *The Transformation of European Politics*.

35. Andrei Lovanov-Rostovsky, *Russia and Europe, 1789–1825* (New York: Greenwood, 1968), introduction.

36. Patricia Kennedy Grimsted, *The Foreign Ministers of Alexander I: Political Attitudes and the Conduct of Russian Diplomacy* (Berkeley: University of California Press, 1969), p. 15.

37. Ibid.

38. Charles Webster, *The Foreign Policy of Castlereagh, 1812–1815: Britain and the Reconstruction of Europe* (London: G. Bell, 1931), p. 206.

39. G. A. Chevallaz, *The Congress of Vienna in Europe* (Oxford: Perganmon, 1964), p. 123.

40. Richard Metternich, ed., *Memoirs of Prince Metternich, 1773–1815*, 5 vols., vol. 2 (New York: Howard Fertig, 1970), p. 607–8. This work is not actually comprised of his *memoirs*, as the term is commonly understood in modern literature. It is actually a collection of documents, letters, and diaries rather than a book of his recollections.

41. Nicholson, *Congress of Vienna*, p. 23–24.

42. Jacques Droz, *Europe Between the Revolutions, 1815–1848* (New York: Harper and Row, 1967), p. 17.

43. Metternich, *Memoirs of Prince Metternich*, vol. 1, p. 148.

44. Nicholson, *Congress of Vienna*, p. 48.

45. Webster, *The Foreign Policy of Castlereagh*, p. 199.

46. Carsten Halbraad, *The Concert of Europe: A Study in German and British International Theory, 1815–1914* (New York: Longman, 1970).

47. Webster, *The Foreign Policy of Castlereagh*, p. 480.

48. This theme consistently appears in Castlereagh's correspondence with Liverpool and Wellington. See his letters in Charles Webster, ed., *British Diplomacy, 1813–1815: Select Documents Dealing With the Reconstruction of Europe* (London: G. Bell, 1921), pp. 189–338.

49. Craig and George, *Force and Statecraft*, p. 26.

50. Sir Augustus Oakes and R. B. Mowat, eds., *The Great European Treaties of the Nineteenth Century* (Oxford: Clarendon, 1930), p. 24.

51. Edward V. Gulick, *Europe's Classical Balance of Power* (Ithaca: Cornell University Press, 1955), p. 185.

52. Paul Schroeder, "The Nineteenth-Century International System: Changes in the Structure," *World Politics*, vol. 39, no. 1 (October 1986), pp. 12–13.

53. According to this article, "The relations from which there is to arise in Europe a true and lasting system of equilibrium shall be regulated to the Congress on the bases concluded by the allied powers among themselves." See Arnold Toynbee, ed., *Major Peace Treaties of Modern History, 1648–1967*, vol. 1 (New York: McGraw-Hill, 1967).

54. Stephen Krasner, "Westphalia and All That," in Judith Goldstein and Robert O. Keohane, eds., *Ideas and Foreign Policy: Beliefs, Institutions and Political Change* (Ithaca: Cornell University Press, 1983), p. 240.

55. See Schroeder, *The Transformation of European Politics*, p. 520.

56. Kraehe, *Metternich's German Policy*, p. 142.

57. Osiander, *The States System of Europe*; and Paul Schroeder, "Did the Vienna Settlement Rest on a Balance of Power?" *American Historical Review*, vol. 97 (June 1992).

58. See Memoir by Frederick von Gentz, February 12, 1815, in Metternich, *Memoirs of Prince Metternich*, vol. 2, p. 555.

59. Webster, *The Foreign Policy of Castlereagh*, p. 337.

60. Nicholson, *The Congress of Vienna*, p. 137; and Webster, *The Congress of Vienna*, p. 80.

61. Webster, *The Foreign Policy of Castlereagh*, p. 229.

62. Ibid., p. 337. A similar observation was made by Nicholson, *The Congress of Vienna*, p. 135.

63. See Jack Levy, *War in the Modern Great Power System, 1495–1975* (Lexington: University Press of Kentucky, 1977), p. 10.

64. Schroeder, "Did the Vienna Settlement Rest?" p. 688.

65. Waltz himself acknowledges this intersubjective criterion by arguing that President Nixon "made" China into a superpower by conferring this status upon her. This leads one to question to value of structural variables such as polarity for either predicting or explaining the behavior of states. See *Theory of International Politics*, p. 130.

66. Webster, *The Foreign Policy of Castlereagh*, p. 73.

67. Ibid., p. 480.

68. Ferrero, *The Reconstruction of Europe*, 177.

69. See Kraehe, *Metternich's German Policy*, chapter 20.

70. Joseph Grieco, "Anarchy and the Limits of Cooperation: a Realist Critique of the Newest Liberal Institutionalism," *International Organization*, vol. 42 (Summer 1988), pp. 485–507. Parenthetically, the relative gains issue did come back to haunt Austria when it ultimately went to war against Prussia during the period surrounding German integration. See chapter 5.

71. Halbraad, *The Concert of Europe*, p. 37.

72. Quoted in ibid., p. 20.

73. Webster, *The Foreign Policy of Castlereagh*, p. 160.

74. Robert Stewart Castlereagh, *Correspondence, Dispatches, and Other Papers of Viscount Castlereagh*, 3d series, vol. 11 (London: H. Colburn, 1850), p. 105.

75. While there is an obvious self-serving aspect to this principle, it was also a recognition that the stability of the Bourbon restoration was highly dependent upon external legitimation. See his letters and dispatches in Metternich, *Memoirs of Prince Metternich*, vol. 2, especially pp. 132–33, 226–27, and 230–33.

76. Harold Temperley, *The Foreign Policy of Canning, 1822–1827, England, the Neo-Holy Alliance, and the New World* (Hamden, Conn.: Archon, 1966), p. 387.

77. Metternich, *Memoirs of Prince Metternich*, vol. 3, p. 199.

78. Kraehe, *Metternich's German Policy*, p. 48.

79. Hobsbawn, *The Age of Revolution*, p. 91.

80. Webster, *The Foreign Policy of Castlereagh*, p. 64.

81. See Schenk, *The Aftermath of the Napoleonic Wars*, p. 125.

82. Metternich, *Memoirs of Prince Metternich* vol. 1, pp. 172–73.

83. As Robert Keohane argues, it is not enough to show that it was functional, but that it was *designed* to solve specified coordination problems. See Robert Keo-

hane, *After Hegemony: Cooperation and Discord in the World Political Economy* (Princeton: Princeton University Press, 1984), pp. 80–83.

84. Elrod, "The Concert of Europe," p. 167.

85. Webster, *The Foreign Policy of Castlereagh*.

86. Phillips, *The Confederation of Europe*, p. 148.

87. Bertier de Sauvigny, *The Bourbon Restoration*, p. 155.

88. Protocol of Conference, between the Plenipotentiaries of Austria, France, Great Britain, Prussia and Russia. Signed at Aix-la-Chapelle, November 15, 1818. René Albrecht-Carrie, ed., *The Concert of Europe* (New York: Walker, 1968), document 3.

89. Declaration of the Five Cabinets, Signed at Aix-la-Chapelle, November 15, 1818. Albrecht-Carrie, *The Concert of Europe*, document 4.

90. Memoir by Friedrich Gentz, Aix-La-Chapelle, November 1918, Metternich, *Memoirs of Prince Metternich*, vol. 3, pp. 191 and 194.

91. This phrase is from Elrod, "The Concert of Europe," p. 167.

92. See, for example, Stephen Krasner, "Sovereignty, Regimes and Human Rights," in Stephen Krasner and Volker Rittberger, eds., *Regimes and International Theory* (Oxford: Oxford University Press, 1993).

93. See the essays by Arthur Stein and Robert Keohane in Stephen Krasner, ed., *International Regimes* (Ithaca: Cornell University Press, 1983).

94. For the distinction between regulative and constitutive norms, see John Heritage, "Ethnomethodology," in Anthony Giddens and John Turner, *Social Theory Today* (Palo Alto: Stanford University Press, 1987), pp. 240–44.

95. Elrod, "The Concert of Europe,," p. 164.

96. Robert Jervis, "A Political Science Perspective on the Balance of Power and the Concert," *American Historical Review*, vol. 97, no. 3 (June 1992), p. 723.

97. The Carlsbad decrees were issued by Austria and Prussia to combat liberalism and student radicalism in the German Confederation by suppressing free expression throughout the Bund. See Schroeder, *The Transformation of European Politics*, pp. 599–606.

98. Elrod, "The Concert of Europe,," p. 166.

99. For an overview of great power involvement in Greek independence, see Harold Temperley, *The Foreign Policy of Canning*; Schroeder, *The Transformation of European Politics* and *Metternich's Diplomacy at Its Zenith: 1820–1823* (New York: Greenwood, 1962); and Ward and Gooch, *The Cambridge History of British Foreign Policy*.

100. Quoted in Elrod, "The Concert of Europe," p. 164.

101. Charles Breunig, *The Age of Revolution and Reaction: 1789–1850* (New York: Norton, 1970), p. 143.

102. Ward and Gooch, *The Cambridge History of British Foreign Policy*, p. 95; Schroeder, *The Transformation of European Politics*, p. 620.

103. Lovanov-Rostovsky, *Russia and Europe*, p. 421.

104. Ward and Gooch, *The Cambridge History of British Foreign Policy*, p. 87.

105. Schroeder, *The Transformation of European Politics*, p. 621.

106. Oakes and Mowat, *The Great European Treaties of the Nineteenth Century*, p. 35.

107. Ibid., p. 189.

108. At least this is the view of Paul Schroeder in *Metternich's Diplomacy at Its Zenith*, p. 6.

109. Ward and Gooch, *The Cambridge History of British Foreign Policy*, p. 35.

110. Oakes and Mowat, *The Great European Treaties of the Nineteenth Century*, p. 36.

111. Phillips, *The Confederation of Europe*, p. 142.

112. Alan Palmer, *Metternich* (New York: Harper and Row, 1972), p. 153.

113. Metternich to Prince Wittgenstein, Prussian Minister of State, November 14, 1818, Enclosure no. 1, Metternich, *Memoirs of Prince Metternich*, vol. 3, p. 199.

114. Metternich to the Emperor Alexander, Troppau, December 15, 1820, Metternich, *Memoirs of Prince Metternich*, vol. 3, p. 471.

115. Ibid., pp. 473 and 475.

116. Metternich to the Emperor Alexander, a private Memorandum on the Formation of a Central Commission of the Northern Powers in Vienna, 1823, 1820, Metternich, *Memoirs of Prince Metternich*, vol. 3, p. 672.

117. Realist historians, such as Bertier de Sauvigny and Henry Kissinger, argue that Metternich was simply a master manipulator who tailored his philosophy to whomever he was trying to sway, in this case, Tsar Alexander.

118. Kissinger, *A World Restored*, p. 217.

119. Webster, *The Foreign Policy of Castlereagh*, pp. 226–36; Kissinger, *A World Restored*, pp. 26–27; Schroeder, *Metternich's Diplomacy at Its Zenith*, p. 26.

120. Webster, *The Foreign Policy of Castlereagh*, pp. 50–51.

121. Schroeder, *The Transformation of European Politics*, p. 609.

122. Webster, *The Foreign Policy of Castlereagh*, p. 151; and Ward and Gooch, *The Cambridge History of British Foreign Policy*, p. 29.

123. Schroeder, *Metternich's Diplomacy at Its Zenith*, pp. 54–55.

124. See the "Preliminary Protocol of Troppau, presented by Metternich to the Congress of the Powers at Troppau, November 15, 1820," in Mack Walker, ed., *Metternich's Europe*, p. 127.

125. Metternich, *Memoirs of Prince Metternich*, vol. 3, p. 175.

126. Halbraad, *The Concert of Europe*, p. 30.

127. See Lord Castlereagh's Confidential State Paper of May 5, 1820, printed in appendix A of Ward and Gooch, *The Cambridge History of British Foreign Policy*, p. 623.

128. Schroeder, *Metternich's Diplomacy at Its Zenith*,

129. Quoted in Bertier de Sauvigny, *The Bourbon Restoration*, pp. 148–9. Emphasis mine.

130. Halbraad, *The Concert of Europe*, p. 22.

131. Ibid.

132. Quoted in Lovanov-Rostovsky, *Russia and Europe*, p. 394.

133. See Bertier de Sauvigny, *Metternich and His Times*, p. 145.

134. Extracts from Metternich's private letters, March 15, 1821, in Metternich, *Memoirs of Prince Metternich*, vol. 3, p. 490.

135. Schroeder, *The Transformation of European Politics*, p. 613.

136. Schroeder, *Metternich's Diplomacy at Its Zenith*, p. 219.

137. Bertier de Sauvigny, *The Bourbon Restoration*, p. 189.

138. Roger Bullen, "Russia and the Eastern Question, 1821–41," in Sked, *Europe's Balance of Power*, p. 64; Schroeder, *The Transformation of European Politics*, p. 624.

139. Irby Nichols, *The European Pentarchy and the Congress of Verona: 1822* (The Hague: Nijhoff, 1971), pp. 34–36.

140. Ibid., p. 89.

141. Ibid., p. 85.

142. Schroeder, *Metternich's Diplomacy at Its Zenith*, p. 222.

143. Ibid., p. 212.

144. Metternich, *Memoirs of Prince Metternich*, vol. 3, p. 651.

145. Britain did not support the intervention, but did not attempt to stop the French from invading.

146. For the bipolarity argument, see Enno Kraehe, "A Bipolar Balance of Power," *American Historical Review*, vol. 97 (June 1992), pp. 707–15; Schroeder, "Did the Vienna Settlement Rest?"; and F. R. Bridge and Roger Bullen, *The Great Powers and the European States System* (Oxford: Westview, 1980).

147. See Alan Sked, *The Decline and Fall of the Habsburg Empire: 1815–1918* (New York: Longman, 1989), pp. 18–23.

4. Constructing a Pan-Italian Community

1. Robert Jervis in "From Balance to Concert: A Study of International Security Cooperation," in Kenneth Oye, ed., *Cooperation Under Anarchy* (Princeton: Princeton University Press, 1985).

2. See A. J. P. Taylor, *The Struggle for Mastery in Europe, 1848–1918* (Oxford: Oxford University Press, 1954), preface.

3. For a sample of the literature on the 1848 revolutions, see Priscilla Robertson, *Revolutions of 1848: A Social History* (Princeton: Princeton University Press, 1971); Peter Sterns, *1848: The Revolutionary Tide in Europe* (New York: Norton, 1974); Frank Eyck, *The Revolutions of 1848–49* (New York: Barnes and Noble, 1972); and

see David Ward, 1848: *The Fall of Metternich and the Year of Revolution* (New York: Weybright and Talley, 1970).

4. See Ward, *1848*.

5. See, for example, Kenneth Waltz, *Theory of International Politics* (New York: Random House, 1979), pp. 105–7.

6. Richard Metternich, ed., *Memoirs of Prince Metternich: 1773–1815*, 5 vols., vol. 2 (New York: Howard Fertig, 1970), p. 188.

7. See, for example, Karl Deutsch et al., *Political Community and the North Atlantic Area* (Princeton: Princeton University Press, 1957).

8. Some refer to this as explanation as a "dual revolution" where economic changes lead to political transformation.

9. See Spencer Di Scala, *Italy: From Revolution to Republic* (Boulder: Westview, 1995), p. 76.

10. The recent thrust of Italian historiography is to reject any substantive link between economic change and political unification. Recent research shows that the objective of creating a large national state was not part of the plans of the major economic groups in Italy at the time and even less among the urban and rural poor. See Lucy Riall, *The Italian Risorgimento: State, Society, and National Unification* (New York: Routledge, 1994), chapter 4.

11. Bolton King is a good example of a generation of risorgimento historians who take this position. See his *A History of Italian Unity: Being a Political History of Italy From 1814–1871*, vol. 1 (New York: Russell and Russell, 1924 [1899]).

12. Derek Beales, *The Risorgimento and the Unification of Italy* (New York: Barnes and Noble, 1971), p. 30.

13. Edgar Holt, *Risorgimento: The Making of Italy, 1815–1870* (London: Macmillan, 1970), p. 22.

14. King, *A History of Italian Unity*, vol. 1, pp. 99–100.

15. Denis Mack Smith, ed., *The Making of Italy, 1796–1870* (New York: Walker, 1968).

16. The historical literature on the unification of Italy in the nineteenth century routinely refers to the risorgimento as the process through which unity was achieved, although there is considerable disagreement over when the process began and when it ended. For a good review of the historical debates, see Harry Hearder, *Italy in the Age of the Risorgimento, 1790–1870* (New York: Longman, 1983), part 1.

17. See the discussion of these approaches in Riall, *The Italian Risorgimento*, pp. 63–66. The Piedmont-expansionist thesis is also well argued in Frank J. Coppa, *The Italian Wars of Independence* (New York: Longman, 1992).

18. See, for example, John Breuilly, *Nationalism and the State* (Chicago: University of Chicago Press, 1994), pp. 96–114.

19. Paul Schroeder, "The Nineteenth-Century International System: Changes in the Structure," *World Politics*, vol. 39, no. 1 (October 1986), p. 23.

20. Holt, *Risorgimento*, p. 38; and Stuart Woolf, *A History of Modern Italy, 1700–1860: The Social Constraints of Political Change* (London and New York: Methuen, 1979), p. 239.

21. T. C. Hansard, *The Parliamentary Debates From 1813 to the Present Time*, vol. 29 (London, 1815), p. 398.

22. Ward, *1848*, p. 84

23. Hannah Alice Straus, *The Attitude of the Congress of Vienna Toward Nationalism in Germany, Italy, and Poland* (New York: Columbia University Press, 1949), p. 92.

24. Vincenzo Gioberti, "Del Primato Morale e Civile Degli Italiani," in Smith, *The Making of Italy*, p. 81.

25. Ibid, p. 82.

26. For a good discussion of the distinction ethnic and civic nationalism, see Rogers Brubaker, *Citizenship and Nationhood in France and Germany* (Cambridge: Harvard University Press, 1992).

27. Quoted in G. F. H. Berkeley, *Italy in the Making: 1815–1846* (Cambridge: Cambridge University Press, 1968 [1932]), p. 12.

28. Smith, *The Making of Italy*, p. 41.

29. Berkeley, *Italy in the Making*, p. 13.

30. Napoleon was born in Corsica, which was part of Italy. Notation mine.

31. Smith, *The Making of Italy*, p. 224–25.

32. See the discussion of Piedmont's reform movement in Di Scala, *Italy*, pp. 95–98.

33. See Paul Schroeder, *The Transformation of European Politics, 1763–1848* (New York: Oxford University Press, 1994).

34. Coppa, *The Italian Wars of Independence*, chapter 1; Straus, *The Attitude of the Congress of Vienna*; King, *A History of Italian Unity*, p. 2.

35. See Woolf, *A History of Modern Italy*, chapter 1.

36. This is consistent with Theda Skocpol's thesis that social revolutions are more likely in countries where the state structures are weak. See her *States and Social Revolution* (Cambridge: Cambridge University Press, 1979).

37. Compare this situation to that of the Arab states as discussed by Michael Barnett in "Sovereignty, Nationalism, and Regional Order in the Arab State System," *International Organization*, vol. 49, no. 3 (Summer 1995).

38. King, *A History of Italian Unity*, vol. 1, p. 150.

39. Smith, *The Making of Italy*, p. 93.

40. Denis Mack Smith, *Victor Emmanuel, Cavour and the Risorgimento* (New York: Oxford University Press, 1971), p. 3.

41. Smith, *The Making of Italy*, p. 58.

42. King, *A History of Italian Unity*, vol. 1, p. 151.

43. Clara Lovett, *The Democratic Movement in Italy: 1830–1876* (Cambridge: Harvard University Press, 1982), p. 9.

44. Ibid., chapter five.

45. Di Scala, *Italy*, p. 98.

46. Delio Cantimori, "Italy in 1848," in Francois Fejto, ed., *The Opening of an Era, 1848: An Historical Symposium* (New York: Howard Fertig, 1966 [1948]), p. 119.

47. J. A. S. Grenville, *Europe Reshaped: 1848–1878* (Sussex: Harvester, 1976), p. 47.

48. Smith, *The Making of Italy*, p. 146; my emphasis.

49. Ibid, p. 148.

50. George Herbert Mead, *Mind, Self, and Society from the Standpoint of a Social Behaviorist*, ed. Charles W. Morris (Chicago: University of Chicago Press, 1934), section 18.

51. Smith, *The Making of Italy*.

52. Cantimori, "Italy in 1848," p. 119.

53. Holt, *Risorgimento*, p. 158.

54. Smith, *The Making of Italy*, p. 147.

55. Smith, *The Making of Italy*, p. 149.

56. Holt, *Risorgimento*, p. 160.

57. King, *A History of Italian Unity*, vol. 1, p. 356.

58. Beales, *The Risorgimento*, p. 66.

59. See Di Scala, *Italy*, pp. 88–89.

60. Holt, *Risorgimento*, p. 166.

61. F. R. Bridge and Roger Bullen, *The Great Powers and the European State System, 1815–1914* (New York: Longman, 1980), p. 73.

62. Woolf, *A History of Modern Italy*, p. 416.

63. King, *A History of Italian Unity*, vol. 2, p. 60.

64. Ibid., p. 360.

65. See Riall, *The Italian Risorgimento*, p. 14.

66. Arthur James Whyte, *The Evolution of Modern Italy* (Oxford: Basil Blackwell, 1944), p. 85; and Holt, *Risorgimento*, p. 163.

67. See Di Scala, *Italy*, pp. 106–10.

68. Smith, *Victor Emmanuel*, pp. 203–4.

69. Di Scala, *Italy*, pp. 108–10.

70. Beales, *The Risorgimento*, p. 128.

71. M. Tabarrini, "Dario 1859–1860," in Smith, *The Making of Italy*, p. 302.

72. Ibid., p. 128.

73. J. M. Thompson, *Louis Napoleon and the Second Empire* (New York: Columbia University Press, 1983), p. 132.

74. Beales, *The Risorgimento*, p. 128.

75. Smith, *Victor Emmanuel*, p. 245.

76. King, *A History of Italian Unity*, vol. 2, p. 130.

77. Ibid., pp. 328–29.

78. Smith, *Victor Emmanuel*, p. 245.

79. See, for example, the discussion by Thompson, *Louis Napoleon and the Second Empire*, p. 267.

80. Ibid.

5. Constructing a Pan-Germanic Community

1. Joseph Strayer, *On the Medieval Origins of the Modern State* (Princeton: Princeton University Press, 1970), chapter 6.

2. A. J. P. Taylor, *The Course of German History: A Survey of the Development of Germany Since 1815* (New York: Coward-McCann, 1946), p. 13.

3. Hajo Holborn, *A History of Modern Germany: The Reformation*, 3 vols., vol. 1 (New York: Knopf, 1959), p. 12.

4. Taylor, *The Course of German History*, p. 17.

5. An electorate was an ecclesiastical or secular principality invested with the power of electing the emperor of the Holy Roman Empire (after confirmation by the pope). Its authority was derived solely from the empire and not from either dynastic lineage or divine right, as were the European monarchies. Thus, an electorate was not considered to be a sovereign state.

6. Otto Pflanze represents this basic consensus: "The common view of German nationalism as an irresistible current sweeping down the decades to fulfillment in 1870 is a fiction of nationalistic historians." Otto Pflanze, *Bismarck and the Development of Germany: The Period of Unification, 1815–1871* (Princeton: Princeton University Press, 1963), p. 13.

7. This position is either explicitly stated or implied in a number of works, including William Carr, *The Origins of the Wars of German Unification* (New York: Longman, 1991); W. E. Mosse, *The European Powers and the German Question, 1848–1871* (Cambridge: Cambridge University Press, 1958); A. J. P. Taylor, *The Struggle for Mastery in Europe, 1848–1918* (Oxford: Oxford University Press, 1954), introduction and chapters 2–9; Pflanze *Bismarck and the Development of Germany*.

8. Again, Pflanze well represents the traditional view, arguing that "Bismarck's motives were those of *raison d'état* and *arrondissement* typical of eighteenth-century statecraft. His aim was not to unify the German cultural nation, but to expand the Prussian state within the limits of the European balance of power." Pflanze, *Bismarck and the Development of Germany*, p. 9.

9. Louis L. Snyder, *Roots of German Nationalism* (Bloomington: Indiana University Press, 1978), p. 73.

10. William Harbutt Dawson, *The German Empire and the Unity Movement, 1867–1914* (Hamden, Conn.: Archon, 1966), p. 12. While the Treaty of Augsberg allowed the princes to determine their own religious affiliations within their realms, the authority of most electorates and principalities was still derived from the Holy Roman Empire.

11. Pflanze, *Bismarck and the Development of Germany*, p. 82.

12. See Paul Schroeder, *The Transformation of European Politics, 1763–1848* (New York: Oxford University Press, 1994).

13. William Carr, *A History of Germany, 1815–1990* (London: Edward Arnold, 1991), p. 7.

14. The Federal Diet was the representative body of the German Confederation established by the Congress of Vienna. As a political entity, it had few powers save that of mobilizing federal forces in time of war. Its members were not elected from the population but rather came from the ruling princely houses.

15. Eyck, *The Revolutions of 1948–49*, introduction.

16. Carr, *A History of Germany*, p. 48.

17. Quoted in Bolton King, *A History of Italian Unity*, vol. 2 (New York: Russell and Russell, 1924 [1899]), pp. 57–58.

18. See Helmut Böhme, ed., *The Foundation of the German Empire: Select Documents* (London: Oxford University Press, 1971), part 2.

19. Speech by Heinrich von Gagern on October 26, 1848, in Eyck, *The Revolutions of 1849–49*, document IV.1.G, pp. 118–19.

20. Paul Kennedy, *The Rise and Fall of the Great Powers* (New York: Vintage, 1989), pp. 164–5.

21. Quoted in A. J. P. Taylor, *Bismarck: The Man and Statesman* (New York: Knopf, 1955), p. 99.

22. Hajo Holborn, *A History of Modern Germany, 1840–1945*, vol. 3 (Princeton: Princeton University Press, 1969), p. 42.

23. Pflanze, *Bismarck and the Development of Germany*, p. 129. The distribution of support between an Austrian-led and a Prussian-led Germany suggests that religious identities had not entirely disappeared as a political force in Central Europe.

24. Carr, *The Origins of the Wars of German Unification*, p. 92.

25. Dawson, *The German Empire and the Unity Movement*, p. 146.

26. Taylor, *The Course of German History*, pp. 83–84.

27. Dawson, *The German Empire and the Unity Movement*, pp. 28–9.

28. Roggenback's memorandum on Federal Reform, January 28, 1862 in Böhme, *The Foundation of the German Empire*, part 2, document 53, p. 98.

29. Buest's memorandum on Federal Reform, October 15, 1861 in Helmut Böhme, ed., *The Foundation of the German Empire*, Document 52, p. 96.

30. Mosse, *The European Powers and the German Question*, p. 31.

31. J. A. S. Grenville, *Europe Reshaped; 1848–1878* (Sussex: Harvester, 1976), p. 70.

32. Quoted in Carr, *A History of Germany*, p. 52.

33. Alan Sked, *The Decline and Fall of the Hapsburg Empire: 1815–1918* (New York: Longman, 1989), p. 150. See also David Ward, *1848: the Fall of Metternich and the Year of Revolution* (New York: Weybright and Talley, 1970), p. 229.

34. M. S. Anderson, *Ascendancy of Europe, 1815–1914* (London and New York:

Longman, 1985), p. 102. It should be noted that Frederick William did proclaim in March of 1848 that "Prussia merges into Germany" (Taylor, *The Struggle for Mastery in Europe*, p. 7). However, this statement was made three days after Berlin fell to the revolution. His subsequent statements and behavior strongly indicate that this statement was made primarily out of fear.

35. Carr, *The Origins of the Wars of German Unification*, p. 94; and Dawson, *The German Empire and the Unity Movement*, p. 54.

36. Peter Katzenstein, *Disjoined Partners: Austria and Germany Since 1815* (Berkeley: University of California Press, 1976), p. 30.

37. Ibid.

38. Kennedy, *The Rise and Fall of the Great Powers*, p. 161.

39. Carr, *A History of Germany*, p. 49.

40. Katzenstein, *Disjoined Partners*, p. 44.

41. Kennedy, *The Rise and Fall of the Great Powers*, p. 161.

42. Pflanze, *Bismarck and the Development of Germany*, p. 20

43. Ibid.

44. Pflanze, *Bismarck and the Development of Germany*, p. 297.

45. Rudolph Stadelmann, *Social and Political History of the German 1848 Revolution* (Athens: Ohio University Press, 1975), p. 30.

46. Ibid., p. 67.

47. Holborn, *A History of Modern Germany*, vol. 3, p. 73.

48. Ibid., p. 74.

49. Sked, *The Decline and Fall of the Hapsburg Empire*, p. 152; Taylor, *The Course of German History*, p. 90.

50. Carr, *The Origins of the Wars of German Unification*, p. 96.

51. The conference at Olmütz ended a minor conflict between Austria and Prussia over the Electorate of Hesse. At the conference Prussia was forced to abandon the Erfurt Union and agree to a revival of the German Confederation under Austrian domination. See "The Olmütz Declaration," in Frank Eyck, ed., *The Revolutions of 1848–49*, document VI.1.A, p. 173.

52. Holborn, *A History of Modern Germany*, vol. 3, p. 31.

53. Eugene N. Anderson, *The Social and Political Conflict in Prussia: 1858–1864* (Lincoln: University of Nebraska Press, 1954), p. 177.

54. Ibid., p. 119.

55. Holborn, *A History of Modern Germany*, vol. 3, p. 31.

56. Carsten Halbraad, *The Concert of Europe: A Study in German and British International Theory, 1815–1914* (New York: Longman, 1970), p. 42.

57. Robert Enders, "Austria in 1848," in François Fejtö, ed., *The Opening of an Era: An Historical Symposium* (New York: Howard Fertig, 1948), p. 279.

58. Holborn, *A History of Modern Germany*, vol. 3, p. 151.

59. Heinrich Friedjung, *The Struggle for Supremacy in Germany* (London: Macmillan, 1935).

60. Pflanze, *Bismarck and the Development of Germany*, p. 74.

61. Taylor, *Bismarck*, p. 56.

62. Ibid.

63. All quoted in Anderson, *The Social and Political Conflict in Prussia*, pp. 127 and 128.

64. Kennedy, *The Rise and Fall of the Great Powers*, p. 162.

65. Anderson, *The Social and Political Conflict in Prussia*, p. 103.

66. Pflanze, *Bismarck and the Development of Germany*, p. 168.

67. Dawson, *The German Empire and the Unity Movement*, p. 163.

68. Heinrich von Sybel, *The Founding of the German Empire*, vol. 3 (New York: Greenwood, 1968 [1891]), p. 39. I am using von Sybel sparingly, since he is generally regarded by historians as an apologist for Prussia. Von Sybel was a historian, but he was also a participant in the struggles of 1861–1871. His work is still used because most of it comes from the Prussian archives and thus includes information that was unavailable to other historians of his time. I am therefore limiting my use of his work to noncontroversial topics.

69. Holborn, *A History of Modern Germany*, vol. 3, p. 206.

70. Von Sybel, *The Founding of the German Empire*, vol. 3, p. 206.

71. Carr, *The Origins of the Wars of German Unification*, p. 34.

72. Friedjung, *The Struggle for Supremacy in Germany*, pp. xi and xiii.

73. Ibid., p. 237.

74. Carr, *A History of Germany*, p. 92.

75. Dawson, *The German Empire and the Unity Movement*, pp. 179 and 190.

76. Friedjung, *The Struggle for Supremacy in Germany*, p. 69.

77. Dawson, *The German Empire and the Unity Movement*, p. 179.

78. Taylor, *Bismarck*, p. 78.

79. Friedjung, *The Struggle for Supremacy in Germany*, p. 49.

80. Ibid., p. 69.

81. Dawson, *The German Empire and the Unity Movement*, p. 179.

82. Friedjung, *The Struggle for Supremacy in Germany*, p. 123.

83. Dawson, *The German Empire and the Unity Movement*, p. 194.

84. Pflanze, *Bismarck and the Development of Germany*, p. 123.

85. Carr, *The Origins of the Wars of German Unification*, p. 171.

86. F. R. Bridge and Roger Bullen, *The Great Powers and the European States System, 1815–1914* (New York: Longman, 1980), p. 104.

87. Carr, *The Origins of the Wars of German Unification*, p. 138.

88. Carr, *A History of Germany*, p. 7.

89. Holborn, *A History of Modern Germany*, vol. 3, p. 187.

90. Taylor, *The Course of German History*, p. 109.

91. Carr, *The Origins of the Wars of German Unification*, p. 139.

92. Holborn, *A History of Modern Germany*, vol. 3, p. 200.

93. Taylor, *Bismarck*, p. 99.

94. This view is symbolized by Taylor's flippant comment describing German integration: "Prussia changed her name to Germany." See *The Struggle for Mastery in Europe*, p. xxiii.

95. Holborn, *A History of Modern Germany*, vol. 3, p. 204.

96. Pflanze, *Bismarck and the Development of Germany*, p. 486.

97. Taylor, *Bismarck*, p. 141.

98. Pflanze, *Bismarck and the Development of Germany*, p. 372.

99. Grenville, *Europe Reshaped*, p. 341.

100. Dawson, *The German Empire and the Unity Movement*, p. 343.

101. F. R. Bridge, *The Hapsburg Monarch Among the Great Powers, 1815–1918* (New York: St. Martin's, 1990), p. 97.

102. The war began over the succession to the Spanish throne and was fraught with misperceptions fed by dueling nationalisms. As one historian puts it, France "blundered into a war which was not unwelcome to them and Bismarck, though taken by surprise, turned their blunder into his advantage." See Pflanze, *Bismarck and the Development of Germany*, p. 122.

103. Ibid., p. 492.

104. See article 3 of the constitution in Sir Augustus Oakes and R. B. Mowat, eds., *The Great European Treaties of the Nineteenth Century* (Oxford: Clarendon, 1930), p. 289.

6. *Transnational Community in an Anarchic World*

1. Kenneth Waltz, *Theory of International Politics* (New York: Random House, 1979), p. 123.

2. For an interesting discussion of Roosevelt's plan to establish a concert-type system, see Warren Kimball, *The Juggler: Franklin Roosevelt as Wartime Statesman* (Princeton: Princeton University Press, 1991).

3. The thesis that the bifurcation of the post–World War II order was an inevitable outcome of bipolarity and structural pressures is argued well in John Lewis Gaddis, *The United States and the Origins of the Cold War, 1941–1947* (New York, Columbia University Press, 1972). Robert Latham and Benjamin Miller both suggest nonstructural variables that can help account for the bifurcation of the post–World War II system: ideological incompatibility among the great powers and the differing visions of the postwar international order. See Benjamin Miller, "Explaining the Emergence of Great Power Concerts," *Review of International Studies*, vol. 20, no. 4 (October 1994), pp. 327–48; and Robert Latham, "Liberalism's Order/Liberalism's Other: A Genealogy of Threat," *Alternatives*, vol. 20 (1995), pp. 111–46.

4. See A. W. Ward and G. P. Gooch, *The Cambridge History of British Foreign Policy*, vol. 2 (London: Cambridge University Press, 1923).

5. See David Baldwin, "Neoliberalism, Neoliberalism, and World Politics," in David Baldwin, ed., *Neorealism and Neoliberalism: The Contemporary Debate* (New

York: Columbia University Press, 1993); and Sean Lynn-Jones and Steven Miller, eds., *The Cold War and After: Prospects for Peace*, expanded ed. (Cambridge: MIT Press, 1993).

6. Robert Jervis, "Realism, Game Theory, and Cooperation," *World Politics*, vol. 40 (April 1988), p. 319.

7. One of the best empirical treatments using a constructivist approach can be found in Martha Finnemore, *National Interests in International Society* (Ithaca: Cornell University Press, 1996).

8. See Robert Jervis, "Security Regimes," in Stephen Krasner, ed., *International Regimes* (Ithaca: Cornell University Press, 1983), p. 175.

9. However, "strong" constructivists would argue that structure alone cannot account for these barriers, pointing out that they provide only a permissive condition for a self-help system. See Alexander Wendt, "Anarchy Is What States Make of It: The Social Construction of Power Politics," *International Organization*, vol. 46, no. 2 (Spring 1992). Others would add that structure is not strictly material but also includes ideational elements such as system rules and norms. See, for example, David Dessler, "What's at Stake in the Agent-Structure Debate?" *International Organization*, vol. 43, no. 3 (Summer 1989).

10. The literature on alliances is extensive. For a sample, see, Hans Morganthau, "Alliances in Theory and Practice," in Arnold Wolfers, ed., *Alliance Policy in the Cold War* (Baltimore: Johns Hopkins University Press, 1959); George Liska, *Nations in Alliance: The Limits of Interdependence* (Baltimore: Johns Hopkins University Press, 1962); Glenn Snyder, "Alliance Threats: A Neorealist First Cut," in Robert Rothstein, ed., *The Evolution of Theory in International Relations* (Columbia: University of South Carolina Press, 1991); Stephen Walt, *The Origins of Alliances* (Ithaca: Cornell University Press, 1990); and Glenn Snyder, *Alliance Politics* (Princeton: Princeton University Press, 1997).

11. Some may argue that regime theories can incorporate the idea of a common good. However, if the concept of regimes goes beyond Keohane's minimalist notion to include everything from coordinating fishing rights to collective security management, it loses much of its explanatory power.

12. See, for example, John Mearsheimer, "Back to the Future: Instability in Europe After the Cold War," *International Security*, vol. 15, no. 1 (Summer 1990), pp. 5–56. John Lewis Gaddis similarly concludes that bipolarity was the major factor in maintaining stability in the post–World War II era. See his "The Long Peace: Elements of Stability in the Postwar International System," in *The Cold War and After: Prospects for Peace* (Cambridge: MIT Press, 1991), especially pp. 43–44.

13. The classic articulation of this view can be found in Robert O. Keohane and Joseph S. Nye, *Power and Interdependence: World Politics in Transition* (Boston: Little, Brown, 1977).

14. See, for example, Jack Snyder, "Averting Anarchy in the New Europe," *International Security*, vol. 14, no. 4 (Spring 1990), pp. 5–41.

15. See Robert O. Keohane, Joseph S. Nye, and Stanley Hoffmann, eds., *After the Cold War: International Institutions and State Strategies in Europe, 1989–1991* (Cambridge: Harvard University Press, 1993).

16. Anne-Marie Burley, "Toward a Age of Liberal Nations," *Harvard International Law Journal*, vol. 33, no. 2 (Spring 1992), p. 397.

17. The assumption that an aristocratic coalition of great powers would be more concerned with the management of international affairs than with the application of universal principles can be derived from such diverse theories as Waltz, *Theory of International Politics*, chapter 8, and Hedley Bull, *The Anarchical Society: A Study of Order in World Politics* (New York: Columbia University Press, 1977).

18. Following Deutsch and Singer, stability is defined as the probability that the system retains all its essential characteristics, that no single nation becomes dominant, that large scale war does not occur, and that most nations retain their political independence and territorial integrity. See Karl Deutsch and J. David Singer, "Multipolar Power Systems and International Stability," *World Politics*, no. 16 (1964), p. 390. Hedley Bull defines justice in world politics as the removal of privilege or discrimination and an equality in the distribution or the application of rights. See *The Anarchical Society*, p. 79.

19. Charles A. Kupchan and Clifford A. Kupchan, "Concerts, Collective Security, and the Future of Europe," *International Security*, vol. 16, no. 1 (Summer 1991), p. 188.

20. See, for example, Boutros Boutros-Ghali, *An Agenda for Peace: Preventative Diplomacy, Peacemaking, and Peace-keeping*. Report of the Secretary-General Pursuant to the Statement Adopted by the Summit Meeting of the Security Council on January 31, 1992 (New York: United Nations).

21. See, for example, E. H. Carr, *The Twenty Years' Crisis, 1919–1939* (New York: Harper and Row, 1964 [1945]); and Stephen Krasner, "Sovereignty, Regimes, and Human Rights," in Volker Rittberger, ed., *Regime Theory and International Relations* (New York: Oxford University Press, 1983).

22. Robert Gilpin, *War and Change in World Politics* (Cambridge: Cambridge University Press, 1981), chapter 1; Waltz, *Theory of International Politics*, chapter 9; Arthur Link, *Wilson the Diplomatist* (Baltimore: Johns Hopkins University Press, 1957), chapter 4.

23. Samuel P. Huntington, "The Clash of Civilizations," *Foreign Affairs*, vol. 79, no. 3 (Summer 1993), pp. 22–49.

24. See Gerrit Gong, *The Standard of "Civilization" in International Society* (Oxford: Clarendon, 1984).

25. Samuel P. Huntington, "The Erosion of American National Interests," *Foreign Affairs*, vol. 76 (September/October 1997).

Index